LISTEN TO ME:
Whispers in the Dark

Lessons about Life Taught to me By Children

by
Pam Uher

authorHOUSE®

AuthorHouse™
1663 Liberty Drive, Suite 200
Bloomington, IN 47403
www.authorhouse.com
Phone: 1-800-839-8640

First published by AuthorHouse 8/21/2007

ISBN: 978-1-4343-1868-8 (sc)

Printed in the United States of America
Bloomington, Indiana

This book is printed on acid-free paper.

I want to thank John Henson for the hours of time and the many years of walking with me through this journey. I also want to thank all of the dear friends and colleagues who believed with me that this book needed to be written.

I dedicate this book to Erika, Sol, Joey, Patrick and Terry.

The stories are based on composites of many children I have worked with over the years as a counselor, case manager and minister.

Cover design and author photo by John Henson

CONTENTS

INTRODUCTION

In the still, deep, dark of the night, children hear voices. Voices that tell them to never close their eyes — or else! Voices that whisper, "Cut ... cut ... deeper ... more, see the red black blood run down my arm and onto the dirty floor. Quiet now, do not cry. Hide. Hide. Run. Run and hide. Tumble into the chasms of your mind, where escape is impossible. Go get the gun! Shoot the shooter. Shoot the bully. Shoot your mother. Shoot your brother. Shoot ... Bang ... Shoot ... Bang! Just like TV, bang-bang you're dead." Then the whisper starts again. "Help me. Please help me! I am afraid of the dark. I am mad at all the stupid people. Stop hitting me, don't hit my brother ... mom ... dad. Shut up ... Shut up! Stop the voices, please. Stop the yelling, please. Whispers ... whispers in my ears ... whispers in my mind ... whispers in my heart ... whispers in the dark!"

LISTEN TO ME! I have a story to tell. It is about my life. My little insignificant moment in time is worth remembering. I am your son ... your daughter ... your neighbor ... your brother ... your sister ... your student ... your client ... your friend.... Some day I may be your wife ... your husband ... your best friend ... maybe even your boss ... or your congresswoman ... or better yet, I may be the one who _____.

I am not just a statistic or newspaper headline. My name is not really as important as my story. You want to know what's wrong with the kids today? Then listen to our stories. You hardly ever listen most of the time. Always, you are too busy goin' and doin'… never listening to me. You do not really know me, and you hardly ever see me. I hate and I am just a kid. I am angry most of the time and you do not understand why. I want to hurt you … kick you, punch you and spit on you. I really do not even like myself most of the time.

LISTEN TO ME! I need to tell you my story. Stand and be still long enough to hear me and you might know me … you might even recognize me! Hey! Hey! I'm over here, next to the….

THE ISSUES

Family Violence

Family Violence involves physical, emotional, psychological and sexual behaviors that are abusive in nature and implemented by at least one person (perhaps more than one) in a family system to threaten and control another person or family member. Growing up in a violent family may take a lifetime to heal from, and the effects on children growing up in dysfunctional homes manifest themselves in many ways as children mature.

Reports show that children who grow up in dangerous families many times become abusers and actors of violent crimes. The degradation and destruction of a child's self-esteem and well-being are harder to mend than a broken leg or arm. Emotional and psychological wounds sometimes never heal and fester inside a child only to be seen later in life as a serious personality problem or character disorder.

 Violent, abusive and dangerous families create angry and damaged children who act out their rage on others and themselves in horrible, almost unbelievable ways.

Foster Care

Foster care has been defined as "a system by which adults care for minor children or young people who are not able to live with their parents. Responsibility for the young person (minor child) will be assumed by the relevant authority, and a placement with another family found." (Wikipedia, 2007)

Foster placement of children in America is one way social services has developed to address the issue of child welfare and hopefully protect children from dangerous and neglectful homes. These Foster Care placements are monitored by private and public agencies until such time when the biological family can provide appropriate care for its children. Sometimes the system deems the biological parents unfit and the family dangerous to the well-being of the child (children). At that time, legal intervention takes place with the court system, and parental rights are terminated and children become permanently kept in foster care or maybe adopted (just maybe). The issue here is that for most children in the foster care system, adoption never takes place!

Foster care was meant to be a temporary solution to a large chronic child welfare issue in America. The goal was to provide a safe living environment for children to stay in until they could be reunited with their biological parents or other blood relatives. The placement of children in foster care has been addressed several times by the government at the federal level in recent history: The Adoption and Safe Families Act 1977, and the most recent Adoption and Safe Families Act 1997. These laws were supposed to help children by reducing the time they were allowed to stay within the foster care program, while also preventing the movement of children from placement to placement without a plan for a permanent family living situation.

The numbers of children in the foster care venue is amazing and actually overwhelming for most state agencies. Add those numbers to the statistics we have concerning runaway kids in America, and most thinking people would be startled at the number of young people in the system.

The National Adoption Center statistics state that over half of all adoptable children in America have "symptoms of attachment disorder," never having bonded with a primary caregiver. Attachment disorder is not the only presenting mental health issue children with maltreatment histories exhibit: depression, anxiety, oppositional defiance to authority, post-traumatic stress disorder, and the list goes on. Psychiatric diagnosis looks good on paper and makes for statistics that provide funding for new and supposedly better programs. Yet, the children have been telling us for years they need more.

Teen Shelters

Homeless youth programs provide temporary shelter, food, education support and, many times, immediate drug abuse intervention for displaced runaway youths who seek to find safety from violent homes, addicted parents, economic hardship, family abandonment and rejection. Children frequently run from foster homes as well as their biological homes.

Shelters for youth are complex social service commodities. We know that America needs safe havens for runaway youth. Sadly, we also know homeless shelters are not always the safest place for kids. Each year, literally thousands of children 10 to 18 years of age leave, run way from, are kicked out of, or lose their "homes." Foster homes, youth detention centers, boot camps, group homes, children's homes all offer options of safe housing for young people. Again, these are temporary way stations on their journey to adulthood.

Psychiatric Treatment

Adolescent Psychiatric Treatment with in-patient programs flourished across America during the 1980s and '90s. Millions of dollars were paid by parent's insurance companies, along with state youth service agencies to "treat" teen mental health issues.

Community social service agencies for children and adolescents became overwhelmed with kids damaged by family violence, neglect, addiction, and abuse. The services presently in existence are still swamped by kids with serious emotional issues, while teen crime rates increase.

This epidemic of adolescent psychiatric issues and problems affecting our children's ability to function and maintain some level of appropriate behavior in the community affects everyone. Where will we put all these kids? The number of displaced children is growing daily and the insurance money is gone along with depleted federal funds (what federal funds?).

When the kids come out they go back to where they came from, and the same problems occur again. The band-aid treatment is not a solution. Dangerous neighborhoods and families produce damaged and dangerous children.

Crisis Counseling and Intervention

Does intervention treatment and giving them crisis counseling for 6 to 8 weeks really help, when we then send them back to dangerous lives with feeble follow-up? Follow up? In other words, do we track the kids and see how long it takes for them to come back to the "system's" doorway? Are we really there to help prevent them coming back into direct care services before they hurt themselves or someone else?! Or do we wait until they "mess up" or are beaten or run before we follow up? The revolving door of child and adolescent services was and still is spinning faster than we can effectively provide services. Sure, 6-8 weeks of Cognitive Therapy helps, but it is only a beginning...only a start.

Orphanages and Group Homes

Orphanages, once the end-all answer to the "Oliver Twist, American style" tale, have all but vanished as a result of the warehousing of children in mental health centers ,boot camps, group homes, and so on. However, some lawmakers in Washington seem to feel this is still a viable option for the increasing numbers of homeless runaways wandering American streets and alleys along with the thousands of abandoned and neglected children who end up at social service doorways. Weren't orphanages institutional warehouses, and haven't we as a people grown beyond such inhuman venues?

4

Orphanages — or you can change the name to make it sound more appealing like Homes for Children named after a worthy Saint of Charity — are still and will always be Institutions. They were and are a solution from another era, for a problem that is out of control in our community today. They were and are at best a poor solution for the 21st century's throw-away children. Just another unacceptable answer for addressing the needs of our kids.

The environment inside the walls of any warehouse for children is alien, lonely and depressing. Staff and supervisors are ill paid and often seen as high-scale babysitters. The turnover of compassionate staff is extremely high. As competent staff move on when they gain some work experience or burn out.

"LISTEN TO ME! . . . Damn, you're just like the rest of 'em!"

Are we listening to our children? Are we hearing what **they** say **they** need, when we have politicians and professionals calling for institutions as answers to our nation's growing problems with damaged and throw-away children? I think not.

Just condemning these antiquated solutions is not the answer. We need new options and ideas. Listening to the needs of the children provides the groundwork for new solutions. We better start listening, America! Funding and building more of these "Homes" and "Programs" only keeps the problem — The Children — out of sight for a short time. Many of these children will resurface as adults with abundantly more issues and deeply embedded anger.

I believe the children need to be heard. Those who have lived on the streets, lived in dangerous families, survived abuse and neglect, then eventually find refuge in various social service venues have difficult stories. Their lives and worlds are not what most Americans want to hear or believe really exist. Listen to their stories. Hear their whispers. These are the stories they have told me, in the dark of the night among the shadows creeping into their rooms. There in beds that barely had enough covers to hide in, the tough-on-the-outside kids would roll up into embryonic balls amid thin worn layers of bed covers . . . and cry . . . and whimper . . . and whisper.

Fearful of the dark but never saying it, they leave the bathroom light on at night. Afraid to let go of the conscious moment as they drift between fear and fatigue, they talked . . . they whispered . . . they cried . . . they beat the pillow at times . . . they cursed . . . they revealed the inner child lost deep inside their quickly maturing bodies. Sometimes they would talk over ice cream cones, the sweet stuff, dripping and covering dirty nail bitten fingers. I found that ice cream is a miraculous food that opens hearts, and children tell things, as they focus on catching the drips, they may have never spoken before.

 Many days on swings and at the pebbled shore of a creek, pained words would tumble from their quivering lips in whispers, as tears of release ran down unwrinkled cheeks. There is something profound about moving your play therapy room to the park and your office to the "Dairy Queen". Once out of those rooms with four walls, children relax and simple joy builds trust. And the more you listen, the more they tell!

From New York to Atlanta, Florida to Oklahoma, the Ozarks to the Poconos. Smalltown, USA. Backwoods, USA. Kids caught in chaos running . . . hiding in the shadows . . . dealing . . . selling . . .. stealing.... using . . . bargaining . . . alone . . . angry . . . hungry. . . .hurting....are you listening?

LISTEN TO THE CHILDREN

If you listen, really listen, children tell us what is right and what is wrong with their lives. They hold the answers to our present dilemma about social services — therapy, education, family crisis intervention related to their situations. We need to let the children and youth of our society lead us into the 21st century by listening to them express their needs. The best way to meet the needs of our young people with the best and most effective social services must begin by letting them tell their stories and express what they need. Once we are open to listening, we can journey with our children, into a new century, together exploring positive personal growth and healing.

We are asking the wrong questions, if we ask any at all. Textbook surveys and questions fall short in our modern society.

What worked 100 years ago, or even 10 years ago, may not apply any more. We must listen daily to our young people. The children and youth I have worked with over the past 20 years always held the answers to their pain and their healing. I wasn't always listening. Sometimes I was too busy trying to make the latest therapeutic model or social program meet their needs. Sometimes I didn't know how to listen . . . really listen . . . and watch . . . and learn from them.

After many years of listening but not listening, I think I started to understand that "kids" know what they need to thrive amid chaos, abuse, social injustice, poverty and physical, emotional and mental disabilities. They also know what they need to rise above the mediocrity of a society that has not always placed a very high value on them because they are just "kids."

Answers we have tried to find in studies, statistics and tests related to issues concerning our youngest members of American Society have fallen short. Maybe we ask the wrong questions.

I invite you to "Listen to the Children." Here are stories about "real kids" I have walked with during my social services career. They have taught me more than any book or classroom model. We have been looking in all the wrong places for the answers to our society's issues and problems with children and teens.

The stories are real. I have replaced names and places to protect all the kids. These are your neighbor's kids . . . the kids at church . . . the kids you see hanging out on your streets in small-town America and in the big cities. These kids are yours and mine — anywhere in America today.

I thank all of these kids who trusted and shared with me a part of their journey. For years, I told them I would try to get others to listen.

Hopefully, now is the time.

ROGER'S STORY

"A child asks questions a wise person cannot answer." - Unknown

It was a hot, humid day, and the air conditioning seemed only to be making the air in my office tolerable. Paperwork was piled up on every corner of my desk. Why did I always put the darn reports and monthly summary off until the last minute? Was it procrastination, or just a livid disgust for writing about the unimportant details of kids' daily existence in an orphanage?

Suddenly, a young blonde mop of hair appeared around the corner of my office door. Then two crystal blue eyes peeked in. I tried to ignore him, pretending to do some of my boring paperwork. He was not the type of child you could ignore. Making loud and vulgar sounds, he finally rushed into the room. (Saved from paperwork one more time!)

Rog ran directly into my chair and jumped into my lap.

"Hi, Miss Pam. How the hell are you today? I missed ya," he shouted, using his usually array of offensive expletives.

"Good afternoon, Rog. Did you have a good day at school?" I asked.

"Nope. I hate that f---ing place. I hate that stupid a-- teacher and all the queer-faced kids, too!" he shouted back.
"Well, one of these times, you may have a good day. I hope," I said as he stood up in my lap and looked at me eyeball to eyeball.

Roger was a beautiful blonde-haired, blue-eyed boy of seven.
He had a smile that would melt the coldest heart and the foulest
vocabulary of any 7-year-old boy at the home. We had been
working on his potty mouth from the first day he arrived at The
Briarwood Home for Children (orphanage, as most knew it).
He thought it was a game. We would discipline him, correct
him, model appropriate language, but nothing seemed to work.
He continued to curse and shout obscene words at everyone
all the time. Afterward, he would laugh, and his beautiful
eyes seemed to twinkle like a mischievous elf who thought
he was getting away with a clever moment of impish evil.

It might have been cute or impish if he only used the words once
in a while. But not Rog. Every other word was a major obscenity.
Many times he shouted at the full extent of his lung capacity, with
spit following not far behind. He also seemed to take pleasure
in shocking visitors who came to the Home with his expletives
and spitting. They could not believe such language coming from
the "innocent" mouth of a handsome little boy. Some of them
would ask me in private, "What kind of mental illness does he
have?" Volunteers working with him often became exhausted
trying to correct him and explain why little boys shouldn't use
such words. I really enjoyed the Junior League volunteers as
they tried to cope with him. A good smile for the day could be
seen on many staff faces when Rog, with his obscenities rolling
fluidly out of his cute mouth, began spitting on the gracious,
finely manicured women. They would smile at the first "f--" or
"s---." Then, as he continued, you could see their faces begin
to cringe in disbelief and discomfort. When he would spit on
them, many called it a day, and their volunteer time was over.

Funny, as time when by, no one wanted to work with
Rog — neither staff nor volunteers. His vile mouth wore
people out, as trying to correct him or discipline him didn't
work. The social workers — the psychologist, the school
teacher, the early childhood interventionist specialist — all

agreed the only thing to do was medicate him. Just mask
the problem and he would be loveable and workable.

Melarill and other medications were ordered and Rog changed.
He was a different child. Now, the obscene language occurred
only in small episodes — usually at bedtime or when he met
new people. Then only little snippets of foul language fell out of
his mouth. The bright smile was gone and so was the twinkle
in his eyes. Rog was a new boy! The miracle of drug therapy.

Rog was not all right, nor was he cured of using obscene language.

What Rog experienced before coming to the Home was unclear.
There didn't seem to be very much detail about his life leading up
to being abandoned on the streets by an elderly grandmother. He
had been raised most of his life by two very old grandparents. His
father was dead and the whereabouts of his mother unknown.

When his grandfather died, Rog's grandmother tried to
take care of him. It was too much for her, and he began
wandering the streets late at night. His attendance at
school was sporadic. It was reported that he exhibited
behaviors indicating sexual abuse; however, this could not be
substantiated, and he was not deemed a credible informant.

What reliability could be established from a
disturbed 7 year old about his life?

"Miss Pam," he said still standing eyeball
to eyeball with me on my lap.

"Yes, Rog," I replied staring directly into those beautiful blue eyes.

"Why don't anybody love me?" He asked
pokerfaced and wide-eyed.

I was taken aback and knew I couldn't show him my surprise. It would spoil the moment he was sharing with me. Pausing and drawing a deep breath, I started to say, "Rog. . . ."

"Never mind. I don't love nobody. I hate all you stupid f-----," he defiantly said, as he jumped off my lap.

"Roger, please don't talk like that. . . . It is very . . ."

Screaming at me as he ran out of the door,
"I hate all of you m----- f-------!"

Now, what prompted that outburst I do not know,
but what followed I will never forget.

I rose from my chair to go after the little scamp when the phone rang. Stopped from the chase, I grabbed the receiver. Out of the corner of my eye, I saw the blonde-headed terror peaking around my doorway again. He had returned. What was he up to now, I thought?

He burst into the room, jumped onto my lap and began yelling into the phone. Every other word out of his mouth was obscene. He would make vulgar sounds and scream words no 7-year-old child should know. The person on the other end of the phone knew where I worked and figured something weird was going on with the child. My caller hit a nerve with him when he began to talk to Rog....

"Hey! That's not what you're supposed to say!" Rog screamed into the phone. Then Rog was silent as he listened to my friend on the other end of the call.

"I said stop that. You are supposed to say f--- you, then I say f--- you. Okay, ya got it?" Rog was trying to get my friend to respond and play the game.

But my friend kept reciting children's poems. Rog became
more and more frustrated and angry. The obscene expletives
flew into the room. Rog got louder and louder, and then
suddenly he threw the phone receiver at me and jumped off
my lap. Never looking back, he raced out of the office.

I picked up the receiver, expecting my friend on the other end to
be upset and embarrassed. Instead he said, "That was an interesting
child." I said, "Yes, very." "Where did he learn to talk like that?"
my friend queried. I told him that I really didn't know but with
time hoped to find out. My friend thought it was quite unusual for
a young child to talk on the phone like that, and so did I. So did I!

We had always thought Rog's obscenities were
triggered by a confrontation, but was he perhaps
telling us something by this little phone episode?

Rog made no breakthroughs in his therapy for months.
Medication was changed several times, but nothing really
changed his behavior. His outbursts of verbal obscenities became
infrequent, as he became more lethargic. Sometimes he would
say something vulgar to a new volunteer or staff member. Only
at bedtime when the lights were out could you hear him. A litany
of expletives echoed down the boys' dorm hallway for usually
10 minutes, until a staff person would go in and sit with him.

It was a dreary afternoon in October when I came upon him
unexpectedly. Alone in my office, he sat in my chair talking on
the phone. Quietly, I stood outside my door and listened. . . .

"Yeah, Papaw, I don't want to say those things
anymore. Please ... but Papaw ... people say they are
bad words," he whimpered into the phone. "Please ...
Papaw ... well, f--- you! I hate you! I hate you!"

I waited until he bent his head on my desk
and then entered the room.

"Hey, Rog, who are you talking to?" I asked.

Startled, he rose and dropped the phone on my desk. I reached for it and held it to my ear. Just a dial tone buzzed.

"You know you are not supposed to use the phone without permission. Right?" I looked him directly in the eyes as I spoke.

His bright blue eyes were tired, probably from medication, as he tried to be tough and answer.

"Miss Pam, nobody loves me here…. Nobody loves me nowhere," he said.

"When Papaw had me talk on the phone to people, they always said they loved me. I talked to them, and they said I love you … I love you." He seemed confused as he continued to talk. "Why did Papaw make me talk to people, Miss Pam? I said bad things to them … things you get mad at me for."

"Rog, I don't know why your Papaw had you do that, but you don't have to say those things anymore — on the phone or any other time," I said as I picked him up and sat him in another chair beside mine.

"Would you like to talk about what your Papaw had you do?" I asked.

He didn't look up as he spoke, "Sometime I'll call you and tell you about it."

"Okay, when you want to, call me. I'll be here," I replied.

He slid out of the chair and left the office.

In the next few weeks, Rog and I would have many phone conversations. Real phone conversations. We had to use actual phones with Rog calling me on a phone from another office. He revealed through these conversations a sordid story of abuse. Little by little, letting him talk as I listened, he told how his grandfather used him for many illicit sexual escapades.

Many of the conversations were taped because Rog wouldn't talk with just anyone. His doctor and therapist wanted first-person data to render their findings and treatment plan. During one of our last conversations (before I left the Home), Rog talked about his pain, confusion and what he needed to heal.

The phone rings....

"Hello?" I said, knowing Rog was calling.

"Hi, Miss Pam?" he asked.

"Yes, Rog. How are you today?" I replied.

"I'm not doin' good today. I...," he paused. "My head hurts."

"How do you mean, Rog?" I asked.

"I feel bad today thinkin' about, you know," his voice low as he answered.

"Why don't you tell me about it," I asked.

"Miss Pam, I don't want to be here. . . . I hate this f----- - place," his voice sounded angry. "Sorry, I know you don't like that word. They slip out," he said, his voice softer now.

"Thanks, Rog," I replied.

"Why do I have to be here, Miss Pam? Why can't I have a family? Nobody loves me. Nobody wants a bad boy like me. I hate it here." He sounded angry.

"Some day you may have a family, Rog. Many kids get adopted from here and go to a real family," my voice was low, and I tried to be soothing. The reality was that most kids like Rog grew up in places like this for most of their lives. If they were lucky, they might get a foster home, maybe. But the older they become, the harder it was to place children.

"No, nobody leaves here. I'm a bad boy.... Nobody wants me. Just like my Papaw said," his voice trailed off. "Papaw … told me I was a bad boy … a bad boy." He was quiet.

"Rog, why were you a bad boy?" I asked.

"'Cause," he said, "'Cause I didn't want to do it."

"What do you mean, Rog?" I asked gently.

"You know . . . all that stuff . . . with all those people," he said, his voice getting louder and louder. "I hate 'em! I hate 'em! Those m----- f-----!" he screamed.

There was a long silence between us. I didn't dare say anything to distract him or comfort him. He needed to get all of the feelings out. I just listened.

"Miss Pam," he queried. "You there?"

"Yes, Rog, I'm still here," I said.

"Can't I go home with you? You love me, right?" his voice was pleading. I really didn't know how to answer him. How do you answer any child who is pleading for hope, love and comfort?

"Rog, we will find a home for you," I tried to sound hopeful. But it was a lie. A lie we tell children intending to protect them and give them hope.

"Okay," he said. "But will I have to do those things again? You know, those bad things on the phone and in that room? Will they make me, like Papaw?" he asked in a sad voice.

"No, they won't make you do bad things," I replied, as my heart was breaking for this little person.

"All I want is my own bed ... Miss Pam ... my own room. I hate sleeping with these stupid guys. The room stinks. They pee in bed, and it stinks. I hate the food. I hate all the staff. I hate school and the dumb teacher hates me!!!" he was yelling again.

"Calm down, Rog. Lower your voice, please." I tried to get him to shout at a lower volume.

"I'm a bad boy ... I know it.... And I say bad things to bad people. Papaw said I was like my mother . . . bad . . . bad. She left me with Papaw. . . . Why, Miss Pam? Did she hate me?" There was a long pause.

How do you explain hate to children? How do you explain why someone has left them? Abandoned them?

"Rog, I don't know why your mother left you. I am sure she thought being with your grandparents would be a safe place for you," I lied again. How did I know why his mother left her baby with these old people? But it soothed him. Isn't it the moment we are in that counts, right?? Situational ethics . . . you say what makes the moment bearable, until it passes into the next moment.

"Miss Pam ... I heard some kid sayin' a prayer to get out of here. She asked God to get her a Mom and Dad. Can God do that? Can he really, Miss Pam?" His voice was pathetic.

I couldn't answer.

"Miss Pam, does God help bad boys like me?" he asked.

I sat up in the chair. . . . God, give me the right answer, I prayed.

"Rog, God answers prayers ... not always when or how
we want. But he always listens.... He always listens, no
matter who we are or where we are. He is listening to you
right now. He is working on the things that will make
you happy, right now." I tried to sound positive.

"Right now, Miss Pam?" he asked.

"Yes, right this moment," I replied.

"I hope so, 'cause I really want my own bed. And I really hate this
place. People lie to me all the time here. . . . Just like my Papaw. I
lie, too . . . 'cause they do. . . . So it's all right, right?" he asked.

Why do children ask the hardest questions? Why do we think
we have all the answers — just because we are adults, or experts
on living, or professional "fixer-uppers" or educated saviors?

"Rog, you know it isn't a good thing to lie. When you
get caught — and you will — you have consequences.
The truth is easier." That sounded good, I thought.

Silence between us again.

"Will I ever be happy?" he asked quietly.

The silence had given Rog time to think and feel, not just
react in fear or out of pain. Now I was to respond to the
question of his future happiness. Little people seem to go

to the heart of the questions of life. Maybe they haven't learned how to mask the pain, or how to live with it.

"Rog, many people in your life are trying to help you be happy. Your teacher, the staff here, your therapist, Dr. Lewis and me." I tried to sound supportive and possitive.

"I need a Dad and a Mom … and my own bed.… Please ask God to help me, Miss Pam," he replied.

"I will, and I do, Rog," I said.

"I guess I gotta go now," he said quickly. "I don't have nothin' to say, Miss Pam…" he said with a short sigh…. "I love you."

"I love you, too, Rog, and remember
— Someone is always listening."

The receiver clicked, and there was silence in my ear.

MITCH'S STORY

"Every American ought to have the right to be treated as he would wish to be treated, as one would wish his children to be treated. This is not the case." - John F. Kennedy, 1963

The scream echoed down the cinderblock hallways and made its way to my office. Mitch was having trouble getting to sleep again. It seemed we went through this ritual almost every night.

How could we ever get the demons out of this child and allow him to have a peaceful night's sleep, I wondered? During the day, he was an active 9-year-old boy who loved to dance for any audience at any time. Dance and dance until you thought he would fall down from exhaustion; although, he never did. He seemed to be a whirling dervish of energy. His feet and legs so flexible that he even did those splits that make every person over 30 cringe in pain to watch.

The screams kept on. I got out of my chair and left the paperwork for another night once more. As I walked down the dim hallway, I realized the sound of the little boys' screams were mixed with sadistic laughter. I approached the room from which all of the noise emanated.

All of the boys in the room were awake, of course. No one could sleep in room 401 until Mitch went to sleep. Room 401 ... where staff feared to tread after 10 p.m., a place where, when the lights went out, seemed to be full of shadows and nightmares — Mitch's nightmares.

"Okay, guys," I said as I scanned the room. The other three boys had covers pulled up over their heads as I entered. "What can we do to get everyone to sleep in here?

"Leave me alone!" screamed Mitch.

A staff worker was trying to get him to stay put in his bed, but to no avail. Mitch was pushing the male staff worker away as he kicked and spit at him, in between the screaming and yelling.

"Here, Robert … let me have him," I said reaching for Mitch. I picked him up in one swift motion and stood him on the cold tile floor.

"Oh, s---," he said as his bare feet touched the cold floor.

"Do you have to use the bathroom, Mitch?" I asked.

His head swung up to look me in the eyes. I looked him directly in the eyes with a stern stare.

"No, Miss Pam … sorry, the floor is cold," he said as he looked at his feet.

"Robert, please get Mitch a pair of socks. We are going for a walk," I addressed the staff worker. "You can settle the other guys down while Mitch and I walk."

The staff worker got a pair of socks from the big old dresser all the boys shared. He handed them to Mitch, who sat down and quickly pulled them on. Then he jumped up, grabbed my hand and started to pull me toward the door. I didn't resist. It was late, and the boys all needed to get to sleep — even if Mitch couldn't.

Out the door we walked. Mitch knew the routine … down the hallway to my office and onto the big brown sofa with all the pillows. This time he didn't know I was about to change the routine. When we came to the end of the dorm hallway, he started to turn right, down the corridor to my office. I stopped, and so he had to since I was tightly holding his hand.

"Hey, ain't we goin' to your office, Miss Pam?" he asked.

"No, not this time. We are going outside," I replied.

"Outside?" his voice started to get loud. "Why? It's cold out and I gotta get some sleep."

"Oh, it isn't that cold, Mitch. I want to see the stars tonight, and I want you to see the stars tonight, too," I said matter-of-factly.

I pulled him toward the back playground door. Several staff were watching and wondering what I was up to. I didn't yet know. It was just an impulsive move … to break the pattern of the "Mitch bedtime routine." He was so afraid of the dark … maybe … just a thought … maybe being outside in the dark would be different than inside in the dark?

I pulled the squeaky door bar. Out we went, Mitch in tow, not really understanding why we were doing this.

The night air was cool but not too brisk. It felt good. The air inside the "Home" was stale and institutional … smelled like musty dogs or sweaty little kids or urine-soaked mattresses that never seem to get aired out … and the smell of stinky, dirty old sneakers , left their acrid scent in the air. The institutional air disinfectants couldn't mask the peculiar odor.

Outside, the air smelled clean and fresh. A slight smell of barbeque was in the wind. Someone in the neighborhood was cooking out, I thought.

I led Mitch to the swings. We each grabbed one and began pushing the ground with our feet. Our heads tilted back, and the stars shined bright on our faces. I was glad. They might be of help in this impulsive moment, this change in the "Mitch routine." Could the stars help?

"Well, my friend, what was all the screaming about tonight?" I asked for the thousandth time.

Mitch was a cute boy, all legs and arms at times. He had been at the "Home" two years when I met him. Human Services removed him from his father's home because of abuse. Since he was 2 years old, Mitch had been used for the sexual gratification of his father, older brothers, grandfather and family friends. He was kept in a closet. He ate in the closet, slept in the closet and cried in the closet. The only time he was let out was to perform sex with people.

When he came to the "Home," his charts showed a very angry child. He didn't talk or play. He didn't know how. His talk was only about sex, and playing meant sexual acts. He had never seen television or looked at a book. Many days, he sat mesmerized in front of the TV in the group room. He would sit with eyes glazed watching cartoons. Twenty people could walk in front of the TV, and he would just stare. (Several doses of Mellaril a day contributed to that.)

Despite the meds, music seemed to touch a special place in this young boy. His eyes would grow wide and his feet would start moving. As if by magic, he was transformed — a young Ben Vereen was unleashed when the radio or stereo played. He was a joy to watch.

Then night would come, and his demons would rage. The medications didn't stop the nightmares, the screaming terror, the almost wicked laughter. The doctors and therapists were not here at night; they never saw the terrified child we held night after night or the little boy who had to sleep with the lights bright. They didn't see the pictures he would draw in blood on his arms and legs , with pieces of plaster he pulled from the door casings and closet walls.

The staff had tried repeatedly to find out what the pictures symbolized. He wouldn't say; he just screamed when they asked. Sometimes he pressed so hard, the blood would gush from his chocolate skin, and he would smear it on his face. Why? All the staff asked him continually, but silence was the only answer.

Mitch would "check out," not to be heard from until he was ready to talk. The talk would be something unrelated to his nightmares or pictures; sometimes childish baby talk. Other times, he would sing songs that made no sense ... no sense to any of us.

He was a sad and very emotionally disturbed child, the professionals said. His prognosis was poor, to say the least. His fate? Institutionalization until he was old enough for release. Then he would be given back to society to ...? Dance? I think not!

"Miss Pam," he broke the silence. "Miss Pam."

Startled from my thoughts, I looked at him. He was swinging high into the night sky. "Yes," I said.

"You scared of the dark?" he asked, as he kept pumping the swing up into the sky.

"Sometimes," I paused. "Yes, Mitch, sometimes," I said.

"I'm scared all the time. They are in the dark, ya know. They are waiting to getcha ," he said.

"They? Who are they?" I asked. He talked about "they" and "them" whenever he got scared in the night. I expected no answer.

He kept swinging, staring out into the night sky. The stars were very bright. It was a beautiful big, bright, starry night.

"Miss Pam, why do the stars have light?" he asked.

Great! Another kid question, for God, certainly not me. This
one caught me off guard. Maybe I could "check out" and
not answer him. Ignore his question, like he did mine.

"Miss Pam, Miss Pam, did ya hear me?" he questioned
in a louder voice this time. (Couldn't "check out"
… seemed to work for others, not me.)

"Mitch, the stars have light because …," think quick,
Pam. Go back to all that high school earth science you
took. You passed the course. Why do stars have light?
"Because they are reflecting the light of the sun."

"But … but it's night. The sun ain't out, so
where is the sunlight?" he asked.

"The sun is hiding from us. That is why it is night. The
sun is still out there shining on the rest of the universe,
though," I said, hoping he would be satisfied.

"But it's dark. Where is the sun? Is it
hiding like the devil?" he asked.

I had to think about this question…. What was Mitch asking?

"Hiding like the devil? What do you mean, Mitch?" I asked back.

"Oh, you know. My father said the devil was hidin' in the
dark. He liked the dark 'cause nobody could see him….
That's how he gets ya," he said, still swinging as he spoke.

I thought I would follow his lead:

"He gets you in the dark, huh?" I said, as I kept swinging.

"Yeah … that's what he does. He gets ya in the dark.
My granny told me if I drew pictures of angels on
me, he would stay away from me," he answered.

"Oh, so that's what you draw on your arms
and legs — angels?" I asked.

"Well, no. Angels, they … they don't like me," he said
as he pumped the swing harder and higher. "Think
I can touch the stars?" he asked as he laughed.

"Angels watch over all of us. You have guardian angels,
too. Why wouldn't they like you, Mitch?" I asked,
as I slowed my swinging and looked at him.

"'Cause I did bad things. My father said I was the devil's boy. And
angels don't like devils, you know that. So, I draw devils on my
arms and legs … I let 'em get me. If I let 'em get me, they won't
… they won't kill me. I'm bad, Miss Pam, real bad. No angels
gonna like me or help me," he said, pumping the swing too high.

"Mitch, you better not swing so hard … slow down," I said.

He kept pumping harder and harder. He
had "checked out," I thought.

"Mitch, please slow down," I repeated.

I got out of my swing and stood in front of him.

"Mitch!" I shouted.

Finally, he saw me and stopped pumping. His swing began to slow.
He began dragging his feet in the dirt. The swing stopped, and he
sat there staring at me, as tears welled up in his big brown eyes.

"Miss Pam … I'm scared of the devils … they come get me in the dark. In the dark is when they always get me," he said, crying now.

"What got you, Mitch?" I asked as I reached for him.

I took his hand, and we walked to the picnic table. We sat down. Tears were streaming down his cheeks.

"What got you in the dark, Mitch? I'm listening," I asked again.

"The devils, Miss Pam. The devils got me. Always at night and in the dark they came and got me. They hurt me, Miss Pam." He was shaking now, as he cried uncontrollably.

I took him into my lap and rocked him.

"Mitch, no devils are going to get you any more, sweetheart. You have angels watching over you … just like the stars in the sky. They are watching over you, and they will keep the devils away," I said, as I rocked him in my lap.

"Oh, they will find me. I know. My father told me. I can't hide. They will find me, I know," he said, crying harder.

"You must believe me, Mitch. Your father was wrong." He didn't let me finish.

"No, no! They will come and get me. If I don't do what they want, they will kill me, like they killed…" he trailed off and wept.

"I promise, no one is going to kill you. You are in a safe place here. All the staff and people who help you will not let that happen, Mitch," I said, trying to comfort him.

"They hurt me. So, if I hurt people, maybe they won't want me. I draw the devils on me to hurt me and show them. I show them I can make me hurt bad, just like they made me hurt," he said as the sobs finally made his body tremble.

What kind of people did this to a small child, I thought? Such terror was in his soul. Could he ever be healed? What were we doing for him, really? Medications just masked the pain. Therapy … well, he didn't talk much with his therapist. One hour a week accomplished what? In the dark of the night was when therapy was needed.

He finally stopped crying. I continued to hold him, and we looked up at the stars. It was very late now, far past his bedtime. His breathing began to be steady and rhythmic.

"Mitch, how do you think we can make the devils go away?" I said. A dangerous question, but I asked it.

He didn't answer right away. Then, in a whisper, he said, "Music."

Music, I thought. Hmmmm. He did always seem happy when there was music and he could dance.

"Does music make the devils go away?" I asked.

"I never am afraid when I hear music," he said.

"And at night, what would help you sleep and not be afraid?" I probed.

He was quiet. We both looked at the stars, and there was a long period of silence.

"Angels … maybe angels," he said.

"Angels? What about angels?" I asked him.

"Maybe I could draw angels on me, and they
would keep the devils away," he replied.

"Maybe we might find some angel stickers you could
wear to sleep. Then you wouldn't have to draw them
on yourself. What do you think?" I asked.

"Angel stickers. Cool," he said.

"Now, do you think you can go to bed and get to sleep?" I asked
him as I lifted him from my lap and put him on the ground.

"I'll try," he said.

I could see by the way his eyelids drooped that he would sleep.
We walked back into the building, and I took him to his bed and
tucked him in. He was asleep almost before I left the room.

Once again, the child told us what he needed. It was up to
us to figure out how to facilitate it. So what did we do?

We bought angel stickers to begin with. Then we used
a tape recorder with headphones. We bought special
tapes, and he wore the headphones at night while getting
to sleep. We removed them once he was asleep.

Amazingly, after several months, his sleeping improved and
nightmares decreased. He stopped carving devils on his arms
and legs. His medications were reduced, and therapy was
changed to outdoor venues. Here he opened up and began to
talk — to genuinely talk about his abuse with the therapist.

SARA'S STORY

If our American way of life fails the child, it fails us all." - Pearl S. Buck

Sara was a shy strawberry blonde with pretty freckles that danced on her cheeks when she smiled. Her smiles here were few and far between, though. She was a moody little girl trapped in her own world of reality. Two of her brothers were in the "Home" with her. No, she hardly ever spoke to them. Being the oldest, it was hard to understand why she hardly interacted with them.

After school, she played alone with her dolls, in a far corner of the activity room. Sara never came to my office to visit, like many of the kids. She played alone, ate alone in the dining room, and never wanted to go outside to play with others. She was a loner child. Her brothers, 4 and 7 years old, were rowdy and always in trouble.

Sara stayed to herself with her dolls. The games she played with her dolls were always quiet and secretive. We would find the dolls hidden in many strange places around the "Home": in the trash cans, under couches, behind large plants in the entrance hallway, in a bathroom closet under the towels. She never let any real person into her world, until …

"Miss Pam, Miss Pam!" one of Sara's brothers came into my office, yelling at the top of his lungs.

"Yes, what is it, Willie?" I answered, as I turned to look into his face. He was a red-haired bundle of kinetic energy, always in trouble for not following the rules.

"Miss Pam, Randy took one of Sara's dolls and ripped it up, and then he put it in the toilet," he said excitedly, with a sharp edge.

"Oh, really? We better go see," I said, getting up from the desk and, of course, putting off that horrid paperwork until midnight.

Willie led the way to the scene of the crime: a bathroom in the boys' section of the dormitory wing. A group of children was gathered around, urging Sara and Randy to fight. Two staff members were holding each child. Sara was crying and screaming as she thrashed her arms toward Randy. Randy was shouting obscenities at Sara, while a staff worker held him away from her.

There in the toilet, floating, were a doll's head and dismembered body. A leg and arm were on the floor. Bits and pieces of hair and clothing were scattered about the bathroom.. This looked like a scene out of a "Chuckie" movie with kids screaming, pushing each other, taunting the victim and perpetrator, urging them toward more violent action.

"Okay," I said, as I entered the bathroom. "All of you in the peanut gallery, please go outside."

More staff arrived and began to take the children to areas less exciting, as we diffused the present crisis. Slowly, all the children were whisked to new play areas in the "Home." Only Randy, Sara and Willie remained in the bathroom.

"Willie, I think you should go play now," I said directly to him.

"But, Miss Pam, I gotta protect my sister," he protested, as he ran in front of Randy and raised his fists.

I reached for him and lifted him and placed him toward the doorway.

"That's enough! Out!" I said, as I called for staff help. "Janice, please take Willie to his room until he calms down," I asked.

Willie pulled his arm away from the staff worker but went with her out of the room. He yelled over his shoulder, "I'll get ya, Randy."

"Now, can we both calm down?" I asked, as I took the doll body parts and head out of the toilet. Rob swept up the other bits and pieces off the floor. We placed the dismembered toy on a towel. It looked pathetic — a toy beyond repair, more than wounded. Just like them, it was broken and battered.

Sara continued to scream and cry, "My baby, my baby! You killed my baby."

Randy retorted, "Yeah, I'm sick of watching you hug and kiss those ugly dolls. YOU'RE SICK ! SICK! A SICK B----!"

"That's quite enough, Randy," I said quickly. "Why did you do this horrible thing to a defenseless doll?" I asked, shaking my head as I looked down at the toy's remains.

"It's 'cause of her," he spit at Sara, as he replied.

Sara was calming down a little and glared back at him. "I hate you. You are evil, bad, and mean," she spoke.

"You deserved it, b----," he spat back at her.

"Enough. I think Randy needs a time-out, by himself, to think about what he has done," I said to Rob.

Rob began to take Randy to a quiet room, but he wouldn't go easily. He kicked and tried to bite Rob. Eventually, they left the room, Randy fighting and kicking all the way out of the door and down the hall.

The worker holding Sara let go. She ran to her doll, picked up the pieces and cradled them to her chest.

"Baby, baby, Mommy is here. I love you. Mommy loves you," she said over and over.

After about 10 minutes, I motioned the staff member to take Sara to my office. Then a most unusual outburst took place. Sara stood up and threw doll parts on the floor and began stomping on them, beating the life out of the body parts. She picked up arms and legs and threw them at the wall. The body, she kept smashing and stomping on until it was almost flat. The rage lasted only minutes, but it was a frightening outburst that no one had every seen displayed by Sara before.

"I hate you, Mommy," Sara said in a small babyish voice.

She began to pick up the parts of the doll. Carefully and gently, she placed them on a towel she had grabbed from the towel bar by the sink. When all pieces of the smashed doll were on the towel, she wrapped it up. Then she stood and walked out of the bathroom. We followed, down the cinderblock hallway and around the corner to the dining hall.

She was singing some little song. We couldn't understand it or make out the tune. When we got to the door that led outside, she stopped and looked up at me. I still see those red glassy eyes staring at me, pleading for love. Or was it for understanding?

I opened the door. No words spoken, Sara went out the door. We followed. Slowly, she walked to the big ugly brown dumpster next to the back of the building. The little freckled girl threw the towel and dismembered baby doll into the dumpster with one big swoop. Then she turned around and walked back to the door, where we watched her bizarre behavior.

"Would you like to talk, Sara," I asked gently.

She grabbed my arm, and then wrapped her arms
around my waist. I hugged her back. Then I opened
the door, and we walked to my office.

When we got to the office, I put her on the big old couch
with all the pillows. All children love pillows. Everyone
who sat on that ugly couch fondled the pillows, hugged
them tight, or built a barricade around themselves.

Sara cuddled up and nestled herself among the pillows, like
a baby bird scared to leave the nest. She began to suck her
thumb. I thought she might fall asleep. Her head rested on a
large quilted pillow, and her thumb came out of her mouth.

"Miss Pam, is my baby in heaven?" she asked in a soft voice.

I turned and looked at her. Here we go again ...
another of those questions meant for God.

"Do you think your baby doll is in heaven, Sara?" I asked,
thinking that was a safe open-ended question.

She didn't say anything for a moment and put her thumb back
in her mouth. It was a very long moment, and I wondered
what was going on inside her head. This was what they
called an analytical moment in the therapeutic milieu.

The thumb popped out of her mouth.

"Randy was mean like Mommy was," she said matter-of-factly.

"Like your mother," I echoed.

"Uh huh. Mommy hurt me and Willie ... and Jessie, too," she said.

I knew these children had been removed from an abusive home, where they had suffered severe physical abuse and neglect. Sara had been the "caretaker" child. Since being at the "Home," she had cared only for her baby dolls. She basically ignored all the other children, including her brothers.

Sara was not a behavior problem, like her brothers, and might be adoptable, although agencies like to keep siblings together. But who would want all three? Actually, the issue was who could handle all three children?

Sara would probably go to a group home when she reached 12. This orphanage only kept children up to that age. Then she would definitely be separated from her brothers. Together or apart, these children had most likely a tragic future. It made me sad to even think about it as I looked into her eyes, swollen from tears.

"How did Mommy hurt you, Sara?" I asked without thinking about what I said.

"She hit me with a broom, then with a pot. She would chase me around the house. She screamed bad things at us! Really bad things. I hate her, you know. I hate her. Mommies are supposed to love you, right?" she asked.

"Yes, sweetie. Mommies are supposed to love you," I answered. "My mommy hated me. She said I looked like Daddy, and she hated Daddy," her sobbing almost uncontrollable at this point. "She hated me, too!"

"Maybe she didn't hate you, Sara," I said.

"No, she hated me. I got beat every day. The teacher at school asked me how I got bruised. I lied and told stories, but she didn't believe me. She's the one who put us here, in this stinky place," she said with great anger.

"Sara, your teacher didn't put you here. She told people about your problems at home, and the courts put you here to be safe. A safe place," I said, looking at her intently.

"Safe! This ain't safe! The boys here are mean and hurt people, and all the girls hate me, and I hate them all!" she said with even more anger in her voice.

"Now, Sara, who has hurt you here? All of us want to help you and your brothers," I answered.

"Randy killed my baby," she said.

Oh, no, I thought. We were back to that again! It was time for a reality check.

"Randy broke your doll, yes. It was a mean thing to do. Do you know why he did that?" I asked.

"Randy beat my baby, just like Mommy. I loved my baby. I wouldn't ever hurt her. You shouldn't beat things you love. Randy hates just like Mommy," she said as her thumb went back into her mouth.

Where did I go from here? I needed help!

"Sara, why do you think people hate?" I asked. Good open-ended question for any child.

There was a long silence.

"I know why my mommy hated me and my brothers," she answered.

"Why?" I asked.

"We caused her problems, when the guys came over. She
told us to get out of the house when they were there. So we
went outside to play. It would get dark and we got hungry,
and Jessie got tired. That's when we would sneak back in the
house. She would get up out of bed and beat us, chase us, hit
us and scream. The guys, they always laughed at her hittin'
us. She would curse at me and tell me to take care of my
brothers," she said, her voice trailing off into a whisper.

I watched her as the memories returned. Her face became pale.
Her eyes were blank. Returning to memories of pain can be a
dangerous thing, especially for young children from violent homes.

"She hated me. I couldn't make my brothers
do good," she said quietly.

"Your mother loved you in her way," I said, thinking all the
time that this was another lie. What kind of mother kicks her
young children out to the streets so she can entertain men?

"My mommy was bad. She hated me. She told me
all the time. She hated me and wished I wasn't
born," she said, as the tears began again.

I went and sat next to her on the couch. She wrapped
her arms around me and cried and cried. Her pain
filled the room with a terrible heaviness.

After letting her sob for a long time, I broke into her pain.

"What can we do to help you feel better, Sara?" I asked.

She rolled over on her back and stared at
the ceiling. Then she answered.

"Beat Randy ... and beat my mommy," she
answered without any emotion in her voice.

"Beat them both. I see. And how would that help you?" I asked.

"It would make them hurt … hurt bad, like
I do," she said, her voice cold as ice.

"So you want to hurt them?" I asked.

"Yeah, and then I want to get out of here. I want to get
far away from this place." Then there was a long silence
before she spoke again. "Can I go home with you?"

Oh, no, I thought! Here we go again. A God question!

"Well, maybe we can find a family for you to spend
weekends with, sort of like a foster family," I said.

"Why can't I go home with you, Miss Pam?" She
wasn't going to give up. 10 year olds are persistent.

Think quick, Pam, and be careful what you say.

"Sara, if I took you home, well, all the other kids here
would want to come, and my house isn't big enough.
And …," I tried to continue but she interjected.

"I know. I know. You don't want to play favorites,"
she said, saving me from my own words.

"Right," I replied.

"I'm hungry. Can I get a snack?" she asked.

I looked at my watch. It was almost dinnertime.

"It's almost time to eat. How about washing your face
and helping me set up the dining room?" I asked.

"Okay," she reluctantly said. "You know what I really want?" She stood in the doorway to my office, her back to me as she spoke.

"What, Sara?" I asked.

"I just want Mommy to love me and play with me and my babies." She spoke and then left the room.

Seems like such a simple thing … love. All the child wanted was to be loved, to be held when she cried. She wanted a parent to listen to her dreams and her pain. All the child wanted was a home, not an institution. All the child wanted was to be a child, not a "caretaker" at such a young age. All the child wanted was someone to listen to her, like her baby dolls did. All the child wanted was ….

KATIE'S STORY

*"A characteristic of a normal child is that they
do not act that way often." - Unknown*

Dear Katie,

Loved your letter. I am still at your grandparents' house,
but by the end of September, I am going to get another apartment
in _____. I am still waiting on a job as a clerk with
the state prison here. So, in the meantime, I am looking for a
temporary job. I've got applications into every store in the mall.

I don't get to do much, so I don't have much to write
about. I am hoping to get an attorney as soon as I get a job, so
I can get my visitation to see you. It's just not fair that I'm not
allowed to see you. I'm wanting to get you for school breaks and 2
months in the summer, and certain holidays. That's not too much
to ask! I miss you so much. I want you to help Shawna as best
you can. Love each other. I know you two get into arguments,
but "be there" for each other, please, for me. There's enough
anger between your dad and me. At least you two learn from
our mistakes. Know that hatred will get you nowhere. There's
nothing I want more than to have peace between you, Dad,
and I, and see you both when I'm allowed. It all seems like an
impossible dream. But I can't give up. If I did, that's giving up
on you two. So hopefully, I can be "friends" with your dad and
see you as often as possible and end all the fighting and anger.

I doubt very seriously that I'll go back into the army.
If I did go back into the military, it would be the reserves.
Not active duty, like I was, but with this war, I could be called
back to serve. I don't know. If I did do that, I would never

see you then. I'm not ever leaving you two again like that.
At the time though, I thought I was doing something right!
It was good for me to go through basic like I did. It taught
me a lot about myself and my abilities. So all was not lost.

Well, sweetie, gonna end this one. Sorry this is sloppy, I'm
writing it on my lap in bed. I'm listening to the radio, my music, ya
know. I love you and think of you every day. Write me back, too.

Love always,
MOM

Katie was a blonde, blue-eyed tomboyish 12-year-old girl, who
was referred for emergency intervention by a school teacher
whom Katie confided in about home life and physical abuse.
She and her 10-year-old sister were having problems with their
new stepmother. Dad remarried after a chaotic marriage to the
girl's mother and ended up with the girls when their mother's
life spiraled out of control and she could not care for the girls.

Life was okay with Dad basically, including the usual
growing pains and adjustment issues, until he married. Then
his new wife and her four boys moved into the house.

The blended family had many issues:
- Lack of enough space in a three-bedroom
  house for six children, ages 6 to 14 years
- The girls lost their separate bedrooms and now shared a
  converted space in the basement, while the "new brothers"
  had the two bedrooms upstairs that the girls used to have.
- Katie reported physical abuse by her new step-
  mom … and the stepmother admitted she loses
  control with the girls and strikes them.
- The new stepmother was a strict disciplinarian and had very
  tight religious beliefs that play into her punishment styles.
- Favoritism was shown to the boys, as felt by the girls with
  their punishments being much more severe than the boys'.

- Dad and new stepmother did not want the girls to have any contact with their biological mother; the girls wanted contact and so did the mother.
- Both parents worked full-time jobs while tending to six growing children.
- The stepmother's discipline involved lots of screaming and yelling.
- Katie asked to leave the family and had been placed in temporary foster care, when the physical abuse issue was verified.
- Triangulation issues among Dad, stepmother and Katie. Who will get the most attention?
- The parents want Katie to follow house rules and not negatively influence the other children in the home.
- Unfortunately, these parents used the threat of sending the children away and out of the home when the children act out.
- The family had very unrealistic expectations and boundaries for all the children, plus they needed teen parenting skills.
- This was a very hierarchical family structure, since the marriage and new stepmother moved in. This was very different from their previous life with the biological mother, where there were too few boundaries/limits/ expectations.
- The parenting style was very aggressive and extremely punitive, along with parental language that was extremely accusatory toward the "target child."
- The parents "target" Katie as causing and being the point where most trouble begins in this family system; her oppositional, defiant behavior escalates with every punishment given and, thus, the family is in a constant state of turmoil.

Blended family issues keep many American families in constant states of crisis, dysfunction, and anger, and in many cases, abuse of all types: physical, emotional, verbal, and economic. Many of these parents lock in combat with oppositional, defiant and dangerous children identify the stressors that lead to abuse as something other than a family problem. Instead, they "target" a child as the cause of all ills in the family system. Wrong, I think!

Session 24: After 2 months of counseling, two times per week, Katie begins to trust me and opens a crack in the door to her soul.

I picked her up after school, and off to the Dairy Queen we went, and then to the park. Diary Queen has become my second office … or maybe it is my primary office. The wonders of ice cream!

"Well, how did school go today?" I asked.

Katie looked at me as she licked her ice cream cone. "Okay."

We sat and ate ice cream in silence for about 5 minutes; she seemed to be in a mood.

"My mom used to take us for ice cream," Katie broke the silence.

"Oh, you miss her, don't you?"

"Of course. That's a dumb question," she said bluntly. "You should be asking me about her. The wicked stepmother from h---."

"What do you want to tell me?" I asked.

Katie glared at me and then spoke. "Didn't she tell ya? She tells everybody about me wetting the bed. She makes me wash the sheets and hang 'em out to dry. Can't put them in the dryer! Oh, no. Hang them outside so everybody around can see and the boys can make fun of me."

"You can't put them in the dryer?" I asked.

"Nope."

"How often are you wetting the bed?"

She hung her head very low toward her lap. "Every night, I guess."

"Are you having bad dreams?" I thought
it was a typical question to ask.

"Yeah, I always dream. Can't remember them all, but many I do. I
dream about the cat sometimes. I killed a cat, you know," she said,
looking straight into my face, I'm sure wanting to get my reaction.

"A cat," I said as I finished my ice cream. "Why?"

"I beat it, but I told everyone it died from poison. I took
a hanger and beat it 'cause it scratched my arm," she said
with no emotion or remorse or expression of distress.

"My dad kills animals. He hunts and shoots them.
No big deal. I kill the cat and have to go to the
mental hospital. Does that make sense? No."

"Why did you go to a hospital if you told
people the cat was poisoned?"

"My mom's not dumb, you know. She took it to the vet.
He said it had been beat to death, so I was the suspect, and
then I admitted I did it. I hated the cat. Mom could only
feed us macaroni and cereal, but she bought that cat canned
cat food. The cat ate better than us," she said bouncing
up from the booth. "Let's go to the park. I'm bored."

We left the Dairy Queen and headed to the park. This was
a great spring day. Not too hot, and the sun was out. The
park was very inviting. Katie was very quiet as we drove
there. When I stopped the car, she quickly got out and
headed for the swings. Not many people were around.
I joined Katie on the swings.

"I hate wetting the bed," she said.

"I'm sure it is a big hassle," I replied.

"Ms. U…. where am I gonna end up living? I mean, do I get to choose, or will that judge tell me where I gotta go?"

"It will be a team decision, Katie. Everyone makes recommendations … me … your case worker … the other therapist … your family … you, and ultimately the judge sifts through all the info and makes a ruling. Where do you want to live?" I asked.

"Well, this is what I want. I want to stay in one school, not a dozen like Mom put us in, and that was in one year. Can you believe it? I want friends. I want to eat stuff I want, not macaroni all the time. I want my own bedroom again. At my foster parents' house, I have my own room and my own stuff, and the food Janice cooks is really good … steak and not chicken all the time or frozen dinners. I hate frozen dinners," she said.

Her ramblings were very animated with facial gestures. This was a breakthrough day, I thought to myself.

"I hated living with my mom and all her boyfriends," she said.

"Do you hate your stepmother, too?" I slipped in the question, as she was so verbose today.

"Well, some days I do, and some days I don't. She favors her boys and gives them everything. Me and my sister have to live in that stinky basement. That I hate! And it's because of her. We were all fine till she moved in and until Mom came to visit. Everything was fine with just me, my sister and my dad living together. Then it all changed. I do hate that!" She was showing lots of anger in her voice and her gestures.

"So, you want things to be as they used to be? Nothing stays the same, Katie. We grow up. You are growing up and changing. You won't always live with your dad," I explained.

"I know ... I know. The world ain't perfect, is it, Ms. U?" she asked. "I wish they never got the divorce. That's when everything got really bad. I started a fire on my bed once. You didn't know that, did ya? Yep, I did, but I was just a kid, and I was mad. Mad 'cause Dad left us, and she ... she ... she couldn't really handle us. I stole one of her boyfriend's lighters and started my bed on fire. Wooooooo!" she let out a loud noise, as she pumped the swing higher and higher into the sky.

"Where do you want to live, Katie?" I asked, as my voice, nonchalant.

"How about with you?" she giggled. "Only kidding. I know you can't take any of us kids you counsel to your house. Too many problems, right? We are really messed up kids, right? Ha! Where do I want to live???" she queried me.

"Nope, you can't live with me — my three dogs would be very jealous," I answered.

She laughed. "Ms. U, I just want a family, like my foster parents. They are a family, you know. They got a nice house. I get my own bedroom, we eat really great food, they talk with me. They listen to me. I even think they care about me."

"So, you want to stay in foster care?" I asked.

She was quiet for a moment.

"Nope, Ms. U.... I need to live with my father. He is more reliable than my real mom. I mean, I love my mom and miss her sometimes, but my dad ... my dad...," she stopped talking and stopped pumping the swing.

I watched the swing come to a dead stop as she dragged her feet on the ground. Her hands went up to her eyes and rubbed them hard, trying to keep the tears from forming. Watching this child struggle was hard, when all you wanted to do was sweep her up and hug her and tell her it would be all right. But reality rushes in and you know you cannot promise what you can not guarantee.

"I need to tell the judge — I need to live with my dad. I will try and follow the rules, and I will try not to wet the bed anymore. I just wish I had my own bedroom. I gotta stay here 'cause my sister needs me, and my dad needs me. I know he does. He has to…"

CALVIN'S STORY

*"Give me a child for their first 7 years, and you may do
with them what you wish thereafter." - Unknown*

NOTE: Calvin's story is best heard from his group home
supervisor and his final conversation with me.

Dear Ms. Uher,

     This letter is written on behalf of Calvin _____, who
has been a resident at _____ Group Home for the
past 2 years. After reviewing his treatment and discharge
records, I felt it necessary to write you requesting priority
assistance regarding his discharge from our program.

     Calvin's progress with us has been remarkable. The first
time he was put through a review for discharge, his behavior was
such that he was still self-mutilating and making no therapeutic
gains. At the present time (6 months later), his parents have
abandoned him by refusing to visit and refusing to participate in
family therapy. They made their last message very clear: "Calvin
was not coming back to their home, ever." The stepfather wrote
us the following: "Participating in therapy was an indication
that Calvin was going to come home and that is not going to
happen, so we will not attend any more therapy sessions."

     At this time, Ms. Uher, we are requesting your intervention
and help from _____ Agency on behalf of Calvin _____,
in petitioning the court to order the parents to participate in
family therapy. Family therapy is a major component of our
treatment philosophy at _____. It is essential for Calvin's
well-being and successful return to his world to engage with
his parents in therapy. However, in the past, despite our

49

numerous requests, a court order was never obtained and his parents basically have abandoned Calvin. It is interesting that at this point of Calvin's parents' refusal to continue in the therapeutic process that Calvin turned his negative attitude about treatment and began working on his sex offender issues.

Ms. Uher, we feel Calvin has progressed as far as he can in our program, working on his sexual issues. He understands the concepts taught about sexual perpetration and abuse. These concepts include the sex offender 10 commandments, the assault cycle, the re-offense chain, barriers to successful re-integration to society, grooming and relapse prevention. After a total of 3 years in sex offender treatment, we feel that more time spent at this level of treatment will be redundant, especially with respect to Calvin's thinking currently, that he has been in treatment "long enough." We believe that Calvin needs continued supervision and structure, although, our program benefits for him have maxed out.

He currently attends public school and has been for over a year with no major behavioral or academic problems. Interaction with peers has presented no major problems in the group home or outside the group home activities. Calvin loves taking Tai Chi classes and wants to have a pet again.

Ms. Uher, we believe at this time, we need your assistance in facilitating further placement for Calvin that is appropriate for his present well-being. Our recommendations are:

• Placement in a step-down program; acute care is no longer necessary, as his self-mutilation has stopped.

• Placement program does not need to be sex-offender-specific in treatment mode.

• Family therapy should be court-ordered; a resolution for Calvin is really needed, concerning his family.

• The threat to himself and others is not as severe as issue after 3 years of treatment, but further supervision regarding these issues is suggested.

Thank you for your attention to this case and to Calvin. Please contact me if you require further information or have any questions. Sincerely,

_____ MSW

Calvin ... Calvin, I thought to myself. Too many young sex offenders and no place to put them. Plus the programs for those under 16 years of age are few and far between. Where should you go? You cannot go home, and really shouldn't go back there, as it seems that is where your issues began.

Calvin's story is short but not simple. When he was 12 years old, he sexually abused his 8-year-old stepsister. He had several other reported incidents of sexually acting out with boys in his neighborhood. The only people who pressed charges were from his own family. His relationship with his stepfather of 6 years was fractious, to say the least. The stepfather openly and continually favored his own daughter over Calvin in conversation and actions. He also believed that with Calvin gone from the family, there were no problems in the home or in his relationship with his wife.

Calvin reports being beaten many times by his stepfather for "nothin' other than bein' there." His mother tried to take his side at times but was berated by her husband. She took the path of least resistance most of the time, which meant she left discipline of the children to her husband. Calvin's biological father died in the Desert Storm conflict, so he really never knew him except for stories his mother told . He has no extended family contacts with grandparents or cousins. Everyone thinks he is a "freak," so he says, and the records indicate no other family contacts while he has been in treatment (for over 3 years). A child really alone....

My interview with Calvin was the last I would have with him before he was transferred to another program. And my recommendations would basically determine where he would go — or actually, whichever program that had an opening and would fit his needs.

Calvin and I had been having monthly visits for the past 6 months because the program he was in needed assistance handling his persistent questions about going home. He felt he was "better" and wanted to go home and have a "normal" life. He wanted out of treatment and group homes. Not an unusual or uncommon request for long-term residents of such programs. After all, these are supposed to be temporary solutions to chronic youth problems. Group treatment homes are supposed to be a better alternative to jail or correctional facilities. And I believe that they are in many ways, but they are not enough, and they are not "home."

I met Calvin on the porch of the group home. It was an early, warm April afternoon, and the birds were singing in the nearby forest. This group home was out a way from "civilization," in a sequestered semi-rural edge of the city. It housed eight boys comfortably, and there were two other "cottages" on the grounds, each that held eight boys, ages 12 to 16 years old. They had a volleyball court (every therapeutic home had one, it seemed!) and a basketball hoop. A building sat in the middle of the small complex, which housed offices, a dining room and kitchen, and group therapy rooms.

"Hey, buddy. How are you?" I said, as he walked up to where I was sitting.

"I'm okay, I guess," he replied, as he plopped down on the over-stuffed brown sofa on the porch. His blonde hair was cut in a jagged ragamuffin look covering his ears and eyes. He was a good looking young boy, about 5 feet 10 inches and slender for spending so many years in group homes, where starch and carbs are daily fare. The khaki Dockers and light blue long-sleeved shirt with sleeves rolled up to his elbows made him look like any other 16-year-old "kind of preppy" teenager. Calvin was kind of a conservative kid, always attentive to his looks and clothes.

"I hear you want to get out of here," I said, smiling toward him.

"Ms. U, I need to get out of here. I want to go home. Nobody comes to see me anymore," he said as he put his fingers through the long blonde bangs covering his eyes.

"Calvin, you have been here a long time, I know, but going home … to your home with Mom and Dad is not going to happen any time soon. I know they have discussed that with you here."

"Yeah, but I know if I can talk to my mom, alone, I can convince her to give me another chance. I know I can." Calvin stood up and looked out toward the wooded area behind the cottage. "I know I can make her understand. It's time for me to go home," he said pleadingly to the wind, as his hair blew across his face and he tried to push it behind his ears.

"Calvin, have you been threatening to cut yourself, if you don't get out of here? The director told me you have been making some mention of this again," I said.

He whipped around on his heals facing me. His face contorted in anger. Then he plopped down on the big brown sofa. "Yeah … yeah, I told them I was gonna start cuttin' myself again, if I didn't get out of here soon. You know I didn't mean I would really do it. I just wanted them to hear me and just listen to me! Come on, Ms. U, I haven't done that stuff for a long time, and I don't really think about it anymore. I just knew it would get their attention and maybe … just maybe somebody would get me out of here." His eyes were pleading, and the tone of his voice was very defeated, not angry.

"Calvin, that is not the way to get out of here. Sure they are going to listen to you, but they hear that you are slipping and going backward to a place you were months ago!" I said leaning toward him.

"Yeah, well, I knew it would get you here." He kind of smirked, and his eyes peeked out from behind the blonde

53

hair strands covering his face. "I need you to listen, and
I need you to help me. That's your job, right?"

I looked at him as he pleaded, his voice and his being appeared
more like a little boy. He looked like one of the "lost boys" from
Peter Pan … body of a young man and spirit of a little boy.
Calvin was 16 going on 8 at that moment of his journey. He was
stuck in a place of personal, emotional and physical transition,
and he needed someone to help him become a 16-year-old
teenager, not a labeled and discarded 16-year-old sex offender.

My mind wandered as I listened to him. Did our programs
rehabilitate or recreate or just bandage wounded children? I
had never been convinced from the evidence or the counseling
notes on this boy that he was a sex perpetrator. My fear was the
parents … the system … the therapists. They had all labeled
him, and he lived out their expectations, wanting to get some
answers about himself and receive attention from a mother, who
for all her intentions, had abandoned him for a new husband.

"Yes," I said, forcing my mind and attention back to the
immediate moment. "It is my job to listen and gather
all the facts and then make a decision … a decision
that will affect your life drastically, Calvin."

"Please, talk to my mother. I want to go
home," he continued to plead.

"I have talked with your mother. She does not want you to come
home, Calvin. Her fears for you, as well as your stepsister and
stepfather, concerning you going back to live there, are real
and justified. It is probably not healthy or safe for that to be
an option at this point in your life. You have to let go of that
possibility for your life at this moment, Calvin," I said, looking
directly into his eyes, which were wet and opened wide.

"Then where will I go?" he asked slumping down in the
sofa. "Nobody wants a 'perp' around…. Nobody."

"Calvin, you have your whole life ahead of you. Now is the time
to get an education and the counseling that will help you sort
out just who you are and where you want to go," I said, trying to
refocus him. "We are looking at some other group homes for you,
and I think we have found one you may like. It is a house with
only three other boys … more like a family and closer to the city."

"Yeah, I know, it will be more like 'home.' They told me about it.
The counselor here has been trying to convince me about it," he
looked at the porch floor, his hair covering most of his face, so I
could not read his expression. "I don't have a choice, do I, Miss U?"

"Well, you always have choices, Calvin. Life is full of choices,
good and bad. You can choose to move forward into the new
program and accept your life there as having many possibilities
… or you can …." I left that open-ended, not wanting to
place thoughts of negative possibilities as a real option.

"Or what? Run? Cut myself? " His voice quieted,
as he looked out into the woods again.

"Calvin," I raised my voice and placed a tone of ultimate
authority in it. "You have come a long way since coming to
this program, and now you think you want to flush it down
the toilet, huh? I don't think so. These people here have a lot
of time, a lot of themselves invested in you. They expect you to
buck up and be a man about this. You are not the little 12-year-
old boy who was taken from his home 4 years ago! Get a grip,
Calvin. Get smart. Only you can make the decision to accept
this. There are lots of kids that don't have options, Calvin."

He looked at me and brushed his hair out of his eyes. "I just want
a home … my own bed … my mother….," he replied, and the
tears quietly fell out of his eyes and rolled down his cheeks.

I reached out and touched his arm. "I know, Calvin, I know." What do you say? There are not words to comfort a child, or person, when they are asking for what each of us wants: to be appreciated and loved, to live in a home where acceptance is not a question.

WILLIE'S STORY

"From a child's play, we can gain understanding of how he sees and construes the world — What he would like to be, what his concerns are, what problems are besetting him." - Bruno Q. Bettelhiem

The paperwork had piled up while I was out and about, putting out fires and listening to kids. Now, as the children's bedtime came and the chaos of the day slowed, I began to address the small mountains of reports. Just as I had finished the first of two, in rushed Willie.

"Hi, Miss Pam. Came to say good night," he said, and as the words rolled out of his mouth, he ran up and gave me a big hug.

"Willie!" I said, as I hugged back.

"Yeah ... and I'm cute and I'm manipulative," he said with that gleam in his hazel eyes. His face was full of freckles and his smile got him out of trouble every time he flashed it. He was a 7-year-old full of energy you couldn't help but love.

"Are you going to go to sleep and not fool around tonight, young man?" I asked.

"Yep," he said as he stood back, looked at my desk and smiled. "You got lots of work to do, Miss Pam?" he asked as he saw me pick up another thick report packet.

"I sure do," I said, as I shuffled the papers.

"Okay, get to it. I'm goin' to bed. See ya in the
morning," he said. Then out the door he scurried.

I knew it would only be a matter of minutes before a staff worker
would be summoning me. When Willie was feeling insecure,
he always came to say good night to me. Bedtimes were hard for
him. Tonight was probably not going to be a good one, either.

About 30 minuets later, Sam, the boys' dorm manager,
called. Willie was resisting staying in his bed and
had kicked and bit two other staff workers. Off to
the boys' dorm I went. I wouldn't accomplish much
paperwork, I thought, as I walked to Willie's room.

The staff had him standing in the dim hallway. He was kicking
the wall and spitting at the staff as they tried to approach him. His
mouth spewed filthy expletives, one after another ... in between
the spitting, of course. Sam was trying to calm him down and stop
him from kicking the wall. Willie saw me walk up and froze.

"Hey, Miss Pam ... these guys are hurtin' me," he said.

"I kind of doubt that, Willie. I think they just
want you to go do bed," I said sternly.

"I can't go to bed, Miss Pam," he said in a whiney voice.

"You told me earlier that you were going to have a good
bedtime. What has changed, my friend?" I asked.

"I ... I just can't sleep," he said burying his face between his hands.

"Sam, put him into his bed. It is late and there
is school in the morning," I said.

Sam reached to get Willie by the arm, and Willie threw a
major fit. He did this periodically: kicking, hitting, screaming

and biting. It is really amazing how strong children can be
when their adrenalin is pumping. It took three male staff
and me to hold Willie as he thrashed violently. One worker
held his head, so he wouldn't bang it on the floor and gash it
open. Another staff held his feet so he wouldn't kick any of
us in the head. I held one arm, and Sam held the other.

We tried to use the least restrictive restraint, but with Willie, it
was hard. He was strong, and he could and would hurt himself
and anyone who was in his way. When he went into one of
his rage-filled episodes, he didn't think — he just reacted.

This went on for 40 minutes. The staff was getting tired,
and I knew someone was going to get hurt soon.

"Sam, we need to get him to a quiet room," I said.

The infamous "Quiet Room" was a padded 10 foot by 10 foot
room. Yes, padded on all sides, and the floor had a fairly plush
carpet. The door had no handle on the inside. There was a
Plexiglas window in it, and the room had recessed lighting panels.
We hated to use this room ... but had no choice sometimes,
when the children became harmful to themselves or others.

It was used at night more than at any other time because it was
quiet and soundproofed. Kids could scream and scream until
they got all the pain and anger out without waking others.

I didn't like using it, but Willie left us no choice this night. The
four of us carried him down to the end of the hallway. He spit
on us and cursed us at every step, twisting and writhing like an
enraged animal caught in a snare about to be bagged by the hunter.

We approached the doorway to the room, and he screamed louder.

"Quickly, Sam ... I'm going in with him. He's terrified tonight," I
said in between gasps. The boy was not only strong but also heavy.

"Do you think that's a good idea?" he questioned.

"Good idea or not, he is not going to be put in there alone tonight," I replied. "You can watch at the window, and if I get in trouble, I will signal for the troops," I said with a half-hearted smile. All kinds of thoughts raced through my mind....

We carried Willie into the room and laid him down. He quickly stood up and came at us with fists flying wildly in the air. I grabbed one arm; Sam got hold of the other. It took 5 minutes — I think, maybe longer — for us to maneuver him. And I got him in a basket hold on the floor. Once that was accomplished, I motioned Sam out of the room. Now, it was the seemingly "demon-possessed" Willie and me … alone … in the quiet room!

"Okay, Willie, it's just you and me, buddy," I said, trying to hold him firmly, yet not too tight so as not to hurt him.

We sat there on the carpet, in the quiet room together, sort of. Of course, he was fighting me and cursing me and trying to bite and spit on me, all at the same time. How long could I hold him?! Only God knew!

"I hate you! I hate you! I hate all of you!" he kept screaming in between all four-letter words. "Grrrrrrr, I'm gonna bite you and spit you out!" he said as he made strange animal noises along with the expletives.

Willie had been known to act like a wolf or wild dog when he went into his rages. Sometimes, he would get down on the floor, on his hands and feet and run around like a dog, howling and baying, snarling and growling, sniffing and chewing. During those times, he would only respond to you if you called him "wolf." Why he did this, his doctor and therapist never seemed to find out.

This night, many answers would be found, but not
without some very rough moments. Yes, I was in for the
night of a lifetime … an adventure to hell and back.

He squirmed and twisted, and my hands slipped from time to
time from the sweat on his arms and my hands. It was getting
warm in the little room. All the energy Willie was exerting
created a lot of heat. Drops of perspiration began to roll off his
brow and mine. I tried to rock him, as I kept the basket hold
on him, but nothing seemed to soothe or calm him. How long
would this go on, I wondered, and how long could I last?

"Willie, you need to calm down. Please, son. Hear me,
Willie," I pleaded. He seemed to ease his thrashing at
moments, and deep breaths and sighs began to come as
the obscenities from his mouth became less torrid.

"That's good, Willie," I said, as I eased my hold on him.

Mistake!

The moment I let my grip on his arms relax, he started to
pull and twist. He reached down and bit my arm. I lost my
hold on one of his arms … and WHAM! He hit me in the
chest. The he began clawing at me with his free hand.

"Hey, little one," I quipped.

His fingernails dug into my arm and raked several deep lines
from my elbow down to my wrist. Then he went for my face.
I grabbed his wrist mid-air…. Suddenly, we were face to face.
His hazel eyes looked wild. Willie, the wild "Tasmanian Devil,"
cheeks red with anger, spit into my face. I shook my head.
"Yuk," I said, wondering when he would tire.

Pam Uher

He growled like a wolf at me. I wrapped my arms and legs
around his writhing body. Finally, I had him face down
on the carpet. I flipped him on his side, facing me.

"Willie, Willie, it's Miss Pam," I said, as I
tried to make him look me in the eyes.

He spoke: "I hate it here. I hate you. Let me go or I'll bite
you and rip you up for the wolves," he said is a raspy voice.

"Talk with me, Willie! You are a boy, not a wolf,"
I said. Time to try some reality therapy!

"I'm wolf," he said as he growled like one.

"No! You are a boy named Willie!" I yelled back over his growl.

I took him into my lap. The kicks had stopped. The scratches
on my arm were bleeding, and the bite marks had come
to the surface. Rug burns on my legs began to sting. This
had to end … now! Miss Pam was all but done in.

I held him and began to rock him like a baby. We rocked and
rocked. His breathing became rhythmic and regular. I could feel
his once tense and rigid body relax in my arms. Now the tears
began. Big tears began to roll over his freckles. He whimpered like
a young pup trying to find his mother in the dark of the night.…

"Mommy, Mommy, I'm sorry," he said softly
between the whimpers and sniffs.

I didn't know whether to answer, probe or be silent. Silence won.

"Mommy, why do you hate me?. I love you, Mommy." His voice
was baby-like as he spoke. "Mommy, I didn't mean to do it."

He began to cry harder. Now the little body trembled from pain, from fear. The anger had raged and lost the war to the pain, terrible pain deep inside this young boy's soul. What was he hiding? What had hurt him so much at his young age, I thought?

"Willie, try to rest," I said as I continued to rock him like a baby. The little boy shook with involuntary tremors.

Seconds passed into minutes, long minutes. Finally, he turned his face up toward mine. He took a hard deep breath and his lips opened.

"I'm bad, Miss Pam," he said. "Really, bad. I did a bad thing."

Again, I just listened and kept holding and rocking him.

"I shot her...." He closed his eyes and his body tensed again. "Me bad. I shot my mom," he said as the involuntary shuddering ran through his small frame.

I tried not to show any emotion. What did he mean? He shot his mother? He opened his eyes and looked at me with an expression beyond words.

"She was hittin' Sara ... then Jessie. They were on the floor. I tried to lay on top of them. She kept hittin' and screaming at us. I got so mad." He paused.

I could see in his eyes the remembering. The memories of fear, pain and hurt were there in his mind ... in his heart. A love-hate battle raged deep inside his young soul. He loved his mother, and he hated his mother.

"She hit me all the time. I'm strong like a wolf. She hit me more," he said matter-of-factly. "But I'm manipulative."

I wondered where he picked up the word "manipulative."
It didn't matter, not at this moment, anyway.

"When she yelled and cursed at us, I would growl, growl 'cause
I'm really a wolf," he said as he made his hands claw at the air.

"You're not a wolf. You are a boy," I replied.

"No!" he said and jumped up.

He caught me off guard. Quickly, he had twisted free
from me. There he stood, in front of me. He put his face
close to mine, our noses almost touching. I wondered
what he was going to do next. Spit? Claw? Or....

He snarled and growled like a wolf. Then he landed on his legs
and sniffed my arm where it was bleeding from the scratches. Then
he touched the marks. I stayed perfectly still.... One of his hands
smeared the blood on my arm onto his arm. He looked at me.

"I'm sorry.... I'm so sorry ... I hurt people,
Miss Pam ... I'm sorry," he said.

 He let go of my arm and fell back onto the floor.
He fixed his eyes on the beige padded ceiling.

"I shot my mom," he said again.

I followed his lead this time. "How did
you shoot her, Willie?" I asked.

He kept staring at the ceiling as he spoke. "She was hittin' Sara and
Jessie with a broom. They screamed. They were crying. I tried to
stop her, but she wouldn't stop kickin' 'em and cursing.... She said
she hated us. I tried to jump on her and get her to stop," he said, his
eyes getting bigger and his voice getting louder as he told his story.

"Then that guy ... he started laughing. He was mean. I hated him, too! Mommy said she loved him better than our dad," he said with a harsh edge in his voice.

He rolled over on his side and then got up on his hands and knees. The wild look came into his eyes again. He began to growl and snarl like a wolf.

"Willie," I said. But he had "checked out" again, gone into his fantasy world.

I wondered how little people endured pain. The strong ones create a safe place in their minds. They escape the pain and fear by being someone or something else for that moment. Sometimes, they even believe they are somewhere else!

He growled at me. "I killed her.... I killed her.... I shot her. I grabbed my gun and shot her. She fell down ... ha, ha," he said with a wicked laugh. "I stopped her, ha, ha."

He crawled around the room, growled and clawed at the walls viciously. Then he stopped in the corner by the door. His face in the corner, he collapsed into a pile. Maybe he was exhausted! I hoped. Then I heard his voice ... barely.

"I'm sorry, Mommy. Willie is sorry, Mommy. But I hate you, Mommy," he said as the crying began again.

I went and picked him up. Enough, I thought. The demons had raged enough within this child tonight.

He grabbed me by the neck, and wet tears dripped down my neck. His sobs shook us both. They were from the very soul of this wounded child.

"Let's go, Willie. I'll take you to the big couch. You can sleep there tonight," I said as I carried him out of the "Quiet Room."

I carried him down the hallway and around the corner, as he cried and cried. When we got to my office, I gently laid him on the tattered couch and covered him with my Southwest throw. His eyes were so swollen from hours of tears. He reached for my arm with the deep scratches, bruises and bites. I brushed his tussled red hair from his forehead.

"Please don't leave," he begged. "I'm sorry. I'm sorry. I had to shoot her, Miss Pam," he said squeezing my arm.

"Willie, you must go to sleep now. It is late, late, late. I will be right here with you tonight. I'll be right here in my chair," I replied.

"I'm sorry. I'm sorry I killed her, Miss Pam," he said, letting go of my arm. He fell limp to the couch. His eyes were half closed and his words were whispers that faded into the shadows of a moment passed.

"Willie, I know you are sorry. I'm sorry your mother hurt you so much. I wish…," but I stopped speaking. What I wished didn't really matter and he was asleep.

Sam came into my office, as I collapsed into my chair.

"My god," he said. "You look like you have been through World War III."

"Thanks, I needed to hear that right now. Come outside with me. We can talk and not wake him," I said.

We went out to the corridor. I leaned against the wall and surveyed my battle scars. Wow! They looked bad and felt worse. Bite marks, scratches all over my hands and arms, and one long mark from my elbow to my wrist on my left arm. Sam had a bottle of disinfectant and gauze ready.

"Here, let me clean those bites and marks," he said.

"You don't think he had rabies, do you?" I asked with a small laugh, as I tried to lighten the moment.

Sam laughed. "Not unless he is a real wolf."

"Right," I said.

"You were in there with him for 4 hours. Four hours!!! You should be wiped out," he exclaimed, shaking his head as he cleaned my wounds.

"Four hours...," I said. I wasn't surprised; it seemed like an eternity.

"Yep, that little guy really acted out tonight," he said.

"Are we really helping these kids, Sam?" I asked, as the heaviness of all that had happened caught up with me.

"What happened in there? You've never asked that question before," he replied.

"All these kids want is someone to listen to them and love them, Sam. Just listen to them and love them," I said, as I fell back against the wall.

"We do listen ... all of us who work the trenches," he replied with sarcasm in his voice.

"But are THEY listening?" I asked, as I motioned up the hallway to the doctor, social worker and therapist offices. "Do THEY ever really hear these voices?"

He looked at me and said, "What do you think?"

Willie's story of shooting his mother didn't end that night
in the "Quiet Room." That was only the beginning of the
story. He began to tell about horrible beatings he endured,
times when he would throw himself on top of his brother or
sister and take a second or third beating to protect them.

He told about nights ... in the dark, out on the streets, until his
mother would unlock the door and let them in. When the men left,
they could come in and all of them would run for shelter from the
wrath of Mommy. She would yell and chase them with a broom,
swatting and beating them on the head, legs, back — wherever the
broom landed on their bodies. She would tell them how bad they
were, and how she hated them, wishing they had never been born.

Many nights, Willie would search dumpsters for "leftover"
food for them to eat. His mother never cooked hot food.
Usually, they ate cold rice or Cheerios, and if they were
lucky, maybe some chips. They did get a meal at school. And
it didn't matter what it was — they ate it, he told us.

They had moved many, many, many times. He didn't know
where his daddy was. He hadn't seen him since Jessie was
a baby. People had taken them away from their mother
a couple of times, but she always got them back.

A dangerous home ... a place of chaos ... anger ...
violence ... hate ... and abuse, such violence that finally
drove Willie to shoot his mother. Why do kids kill?

The good thing about Willie's story is that he didn't kill his
mother. She lived because he shot her with a BB gun in the legs.
But to a 7 year old, a gun is a gun! The pellets hit his mother,
and she fell down. There was blood, police, and he did it.

In a fit of rage, or maybe hate, or perhaps
fear ... Willie shot his mother.

Forever he will remember that act. It will haunt him. Maybe he will learn to cope with the fact or rationalize it someday. The question from this story remains a difficult issue for American Social Services: When is a family too abusive? Too violent? And when we do remove kids from dangerous homes, why do we send them back? A dangerous home is a dangerous home. Isn't it??

America reaps what it sows. Who really listens to the voices of the children? Who do the kids really talk to?

I will never forget Willie. It was my last day at the "Home," and as I was doing my last report, he came running in.

He ran and jumped into my lap and said, "Hi, I'm Willie, and I'm manipulative." I hugged him and he hugged me back. But I wondered … was the wolf gone for good? Or was he lurking somewhere in the deep corridors of Willie's mind?

TRACE'S STORY

"Live so that when your children think of fairness and integrity, they think of you." - *H. Jackson Brown, Jr.*

Before I went home on this late spring day, I tried to catch up on my paperwork. Ha! What a joke! My desk was piled high again after several months of doing basically what I had to do: daily and weekly reports and notes on sessions.

The children took priority in this crumbling institution, always. If I weren't running to the store to pick up three-day old birthday cakes or running to the docks to pick up donated food, then I was fixing skinned knees or settling some dumb kids' fight in the hallways or on the playground. Then in between all of these activities, I would be spending time talking with kids (or counseling, as some would like to call it).

I finally got to the bottom of one pile of reports when I saw Trace's file. In my heart, I knew I needed to get this one done before I went home today. Trace was up for adoption, and we had to have all files completely up to date before the committee would review to finalize the process.

This was going to be one of the happy endings for a child here in this institution. Most would never be adopted and would end up in foster homes. But Trace was blessed. The family he went with on weekends for outings wanted to keep him permanently.

This was a good match, I thought, as I started to wrap up the reports in his file. Trace was a slight, wiry blacked-

haired boy of 12. He had been found on the streets of
an urban city in the Southwest, scrounging for food in
dumpsters. He spoke broken English, his file stated, when
he was found at the age of approximately 5. No one knew
his exact age or his birthday, so his B-day became the day
he was taken from the streets by Children's Services.

Passed from one program to another and foster home to foster
home for 6 years, he landed with us as a last ditch effort before
juvenile detention or worse (if there is such). He could not
remember his family or his real name. Somewhere in his travels,
someone called him "Not a Trace," and the Trace part stuck.

Trace was not a really "bad" kid, but he was tough at times,
and he knew every curse word — in five languages!

He was in fights constantly and had few friends. Until the day
the Vargas took him home for a weekend. We had a program
where older kids with good behavior could go for weekends with
families who were "Weekend Warrior Time Out Foster Parents."

The Vargas and Trace melded into a great match from day one.
Julian Varga was Trace's age and loved baseball, which was Trace's
favorite sport. The boys became "best buds," and Trace became
the little brother Julian had always wanted … and the other
son Joe and Susan Varga always dreamed of having. And Trace
seemed to be getting the one thing he had never had: a family.
A family that loved him and whom he loved in return. Miracles
do happen, I thought, writing furiously to finish this file.

I signed my name at the end of Trace's report, folded the
file folder and put it into the basket for the committee
meeting in the morning. Done deal…. Or so I thought.

Two weeks from the day I signed the file on Trace, I was
coming into my office when I heard a blood-curdling scream

from the boys' section hallway. I dropped my briefcase
and took off to the land of "boys 12 and under."

"Miss Pam, Miss Pam, come quick!" the voice of a staff
member was yelling to me from the end of the corridor.

It was Jamie. She and Pete were holding down one of the
boys who was screaming like a wild boar, while kicking and
throwing punches that landed, smacking loudly, against
the two staff workers. When I got to the mess of people
on the floor, I could see Trace was the "wild boar child."
He was kicking and hitting while screaming and trying
to bite whatever human flesh came near his mouth.

"Enough! Enough! Trace! What is going on here?" I asked, as I
went to my knees on the floor and took hold of his ankles. I pushed
them forcefully to the tile floor as Jamie and Pete tried to contain
his upper body, preventing him from banging his head on the floor.

"Heeeeeeeeeee … I hate you! … I hate this place! …
Yeow…Grrrrrrrrrrrrrrrrr!" he answered in an almost animal
snarl-scream-cry. Large tears were streaming down his face
and his beautiful big brown eyes were wild with rage.

"Somebody tell me what set him off," I said, looking
at both Jamie and Pete, and then at the 12-year-old's
feet, which were trying to kick free of my grip.

"Somebody told him he wasn't getting adopted," Pete said.

"What? Who said? That was a done deal.What the…,"
I caught myself before finishing the sentence.

"Janice told him," Jamie said.

"What?" I again looked up from the wild feet I was
trying to contain and almost lost my grip. Janice was

73

the Director of this Children's Program and Home,
and she knew every _____. I'll stop there.

"He has been like this ever since, running around the playground,
crazy ... hitting everything and everyone. Then he came inside
and went to his room with the two of us not far behind him.
Once he got into his room, he began to tear it apart. You'll
see when you go there. We finally caught him and tried to
restrain him quietly. That was a trick! As you can see, he
began trying to bite us and spit on us," Jamie said struggling
to hold his head with one hand and his arm with the other.

"Trace . This isn't helping you. You have got to stop
fighting us. Stop now. We can go to my office and find
the answers to this problem. Trace, listen to me!"

"Miss Pam, I'm gonna run away. I don't wanna be here no
more. I'll get Jules, and we will run ... run far from here,"
he said, as his struggling seemed to be slowing down.
His feet stopped kicking; although, he was still twisting
his torso and pushing ... pulling to free his arms.

"Trace, do you trust me?" Silence for a moment. I believe he was
thinking and maybe getting a little tired of the struggle. His wrists
were certainly red and so was his tear-stained face. "Trace?"

Suddenly, like air escaping from a balloon, we
heard a sigh and his body went limp.

"Okay," a tiny voice spoke. The raging
wild boar child was giving in.

"Let's stand up, wash off the tears with a towel and go to my office.
Okay?" I said as we stood up and Pete quickly pulled Trace to his
feet — before he had time to think about anymore fists or biting.

I leaned over and looked him right in the eyes. They were puffy and wet from many tears but still filled with fear.

"Okay," he replied.

Jamie got a bunch of wet paper towels from the hall bathroom and wiped his face. Pete straightened his shirt and tied a shoelace, which had come undone during the struggle.

(I dearly loved this staff, I thought. One minute they are being bitten, kicked, spit on and punched, and the next moment, they are compassionate and loving to a child who knows very little about love. God bless these underpaid "angels of childcare!")

Trace and I started to walk toward my office. Pete followed beside Trace on the other side, and Jamie went back to whatever Jamie was doing before the rumble. When we got to my office, Trace was breathing easier and the rage-filled energy was gone. He walked in and dumped his thin body on my big brown sofa like a sack of potatoes.

"Thanks, Pete," I said.

"You going to be okay?" he asked.

"Believe so," I said as I looked at the little pile of limp boy sitting on the sofa. "We need to find out what is going on. Will you go to Janice's office and see if she is willing to tell you anything?"

"Sure. I'll be back," he said, striding off to the upper echelons ... the kingdom of administrators.

I turned my attention to the broken spirit now sharing my office with me. He certainly looked pathetic and wasted from his outburst. Who could blame him for being angry? The one thing he wanted and needed was not going to be!

"Trace, talk to me, please," I said as I sat in my chair.

"About what? I'm gonna run, Miss Pam. I'm really gonna. I'm gonna live with the Varga family and nobody better try 'n stop me." He looked up at me as he spoke. "Why they gonna do this to me? Why? Huh? Why?"

"I don't know," I said, and I truly didn't know what was going on. This was a good match and a good thing for this child. It was supposed to be a very easy adoption and transition. What went wrong, I thought to myself?

Just as I was going to speak, I saw Peter walk up to the doorway. I got up and went out into the hall with him.

"Well????" I asked, my hands on my hips and my face pinched into a scowl.

"You are not gonna' believe this! She told me there would be no adoption. The committee felt the family wasn't right for Trace. That's all she would tell me. Except ... well, her words were, 'Tell your supervisor to get that boy under control. There are to be no more incidents.'"

"Really?!" I looked at Peter, and then I looked into the room at Trace. "Why did they tell him yes, and then pull this stunt? Why, Pete?" I knew he didn't have the answer, but I would find out. That was not a good thing.

I returned to my office and fell into my chair. My head went to my hands as I rested my elbows on my knees and gazed at the lost little boy on the overstuffed sofa.

"Trace , I ...," my voice trailed off; I really did not know what to say. The kids all knew my three rules: 1. No lying. Tell the truth; it comes back to bite you. 2. No stealing. If

you don't own it, borrow it or work for it. 3. No cheating. A
cheater only cheats himself out of friends, trust and love.

I did not lie to them. I did not steal hope from them.
And I never cheated them out of opportunity for
love. Now, all these were happening to this little
boy and his life would not be the same. Ever!

"Miss Pam, I hate this place. I hate most of the kids here,
too! I just wanna go live with Julian and his family. They
are nice to me ... I mean, if I get in trouble, they give me
consequences, but they like me ... I know they do. They
want me to be part of their family. Why can't I, Miss Pam?
Why not?!" he half yelled and half cried in anguish.

What do you say to a child in such pain? You dangle hope and
love in front of his eyes and let him taste it, breathe it, touch it
and live it. Then you let him fall in love with a family. He bonds
and learns for the first time what it is like to have a mother
... a father ... a brother and believe he can have a "normal"
life. Bang-Boom! Crash! All gone. Sorry, not for you.
"Trace, I will talk with your doctor and the social worker
as soon as I can. I do not know why this is happening, but I
will try to get some answers. In the meantime, you have to
calm down and not act out. Please, Trace. Give me time to
try and find out what is going on," I said, half pleading with
the child curled up on the sofa holding his knees to his chest
and resting his head on the ugly orange pillow behind him.

"Miss Pam ... God don't like me, does he?"

"What do you mean, Trace?" I asked.

"I mean, God don't like me. First, he lost my real parents from
me. I don't even remember what they look like. I don't know
who they are. You know, I don't know what my real name is," he
explained as he buried his head into the pillow and clasped his legs

tighter. "I ain't got no family, Miss Pam. This would have been my first family. Do ya think they don't want me or something?"

"No, I believe they want you, Trace. I think there is another reason for this problem," I said.

"What?!" his big brown eyes desperate as he raised his head and looked at me.

"I do not know."

"It's me. Gotta be me. Nobody really wants me. I'm a dumb and stupid f-----," he went on. "Stop that, Trace! You are not dumb and stupid."

He started to cry again, only these were not tears of anger; this was sobbing, gut-wrenching sobbing and a stream of tears coming from this child's soul.

"I ... I ... I hate God ... 'cause he hates me. I ... I ... wanna die ... maybe I will ... huh.... THIS IS A F----- - PLACE! I HATE IT!" His sobs were wails of pain now.

I went to the sofa and sat down next to him. Slowly, I reached over and pulled him to me. Trace usually didn't like to be touched much since he had been physically abused when he lived on the streets. So touch was a fearful thing to him when he felt vulnerable, as I knew he was feeling now.

But he melted into my arms as he sobbed. I know he cried for at least an hour, until the sobs caused his body to rail and quiver. After what seemed like hours, the sobs stopped and he fell asleep. Gently, I laid him down on the big comfy sofa and covered him with my grandmother's quilt.

It took me all of 24 hours to find out what went wrong with Trace's adoption. The committee, which was basically the psychologist and social worker, felt it wasn't a good match because the Varga family was not the same ethnic background as Trace; so, the adoption was a no go! (Where was Angelina Jolie then?)

The stupid, stupid thing about this was that everyone knew from the beginning. So why did they hold out the possibility, actually start the process and tell everyone it was going to happen???

Trace had a very bad day after his session with his social worker, who told him definitely he would not be living with the Varga family. And he would not be allowed to visit them anymore because of his anger. Wrong thing to do! She later reported she was acting on the direct orders of the psychologist. And they were supposedly preparing Trace for the future! Wrong!

We had a very hard time getting him to go to bed that night. Around 11 p.m., an alarm went off. I was just getting ready to go home, of course. It was the boys' wing alarm. We all went running in that direction.

Derrick, Paul and Pete found Trace half out the window. He had broken the bottom pane and severely cut his leg. Blood was gushing all over the wall, and the staff was trying to pull him back inside. They managed to get him in and down on his bed in a six-person restraint with me holding a towel on the deep gash.

"Why, Trace, why?" I asked as we tried to get him to calm down.

"'Cause I told ya…. I hate this place … and everybody here … even you! You lied to me! You lied to me!" he kept screaming as he thrashed, kicked, pulled and pushed.

"Miss Pam never lied to you, Trace," said Pete.

"All of you lie! You b-------! I hate you all!" he said and spit on Pete.

"Enough, Trace. We have to get you to the hospital and you are going to calm down now!" I said, my tone was more than stern. The fighting was causing the deep cut to bleed profusely.

"No … no," he kept fighting.

I turned to Derrick, "Go to my office and call Dr. Keystone. Tell him we need a sedative and to get down here and help us."

"You want me to call him at this hour?" Derrick replied. He was very apprehensive because he and Dr. Keystone had had several conflicts about kids in the past. Calling them "conflicts" is putting it nicely.

"Oh … no, Kelly, you go call. Derrick and the doctor do not see eye to eye very often," I said.

"Sure," she replied.

Two hours after we left a message for the great psychiatrist, he had his answering service call. We were already at the hospital with Trace.

They stitched him up and gave him a shot of Haladol to help him sleep through the night. We drove back to the children's home. Pete carried Trace in and put him to bed. It was 4 a.m., and I finally went home, exhausted.

I went to work 2 hours later than usual the next day. What happened that afternoon has haunted me forever, and it is part of the reason I write this book.

I went to my office, dropped off my things and started to read my messages, when I heard someone screaming. Oh, here we go again. Who is it this time? I got up out of my chair and headed down the cinderblock hallway, letting my ears guide me.

"HELLLLLLLLP! Let me go! HELLLLLLLLLP!"
the voice screamed from the boys' wing. Oh, no! It's
probably Trace, I thought. I pushed the swinging
doors open and walked onto the unit.

There was Trace being carried down the hallway by two orderlies
dressed in whites toward the exit doorway. Trace was covered up
… no… Trace was in a straight-jacket! I could not believe my eyes!

I started to run down the hall toward them. "Hey, where are
you going with that boy?" I yelled at the men in white.

As I yelled, the shaggy black-haired boy
tossed his head back and saw me.

"Miss Pam! Miss Pam! Please don't let them take
me … Miss Pam! Please! I'll be good … please,
Miss Pam!" cried Trace in a voice of terror.

I was halfway to them when Pete caught me by
the arm and stopped me dead in my run.

"Let them go," he said quietly. "You have no control
over this. We already tried to stop them from taking
him out like this. Keystone ordered it."

I looked at Pete in disbelief. "What?"

"Yeah, after the hospital deal, he said he wanted the 'psycho'
kid out of here. He will influence other kids, he said. They
are taking him to the state mental hospital for kids," he
said. He hung his head after he spoke these words.

"Damn … Damn….," was all I could say.

The men in white carried Trace out the door as he
continued to scream, "Please, Miss Pam…. Please,

Miss Pam, help me!!! Help me, Miss Pam!!!" The door slammed shut, and I didn't hear the voice anymore.

But I hear the voice in my head almost every day. It never stops pleading and calling my name.

Most times when things like this happen in children's services, you never know what happens to the child. This time, I did see Trace one more time, many years later. I was at my mother's house reading one of those gossip tabloids she had on the table. There was a section about kids up for adoption, and Trace's face popped out at me. He was "ready" for adoption, the article reported, now 17 years old and in need of a family. His stay at the state mental hospital would be finished when he was 18.

My heart stopped again for a moment that afternoon, reading his story. He once had a family who wanted him ... who loved him. Fools! We are worse than fools with all our psychological jargon and theories of what kids need and what is best.

I just wish I didn't hear his voice, begging me...

Jasmine's Story

"Remember that each child is a separate person, yours forever, but never fully yours. She can never be all you wished or wanted, or all you know she could be. But she will be a better human being if you can let her be herself." - Stella Chess

Jasmine, or "Jazzy" as we called her, was 11 years old and very tall for her age, all legs, and at that self-conscious stage of growth. She would trip over her own feet and get wrapped up in her lanky legs two or three times a day. The other kids teased her without mercy.

Her hair always bothered her — either her barrettes were the wrong color or her braids were crooked. Young African American girls' hair didn't get the attention it needed in the "Home." Few of the staff knew how to fix it, and those who did really didn't have the time while trying to get 40 girls ready for school each morning.

Jazzy always looked nice though. Her outfits were crisp and colorful, and color coordinated. She wanted to look nice — after all, she was beginning to notice the boys!

The Jazzy story….her history before the home was a classic tale from the "A Files." Abused by her father, sexually … abused by her grandfather ,sexually … and scorned by her mother, who allowed the abuse to avoid physical abuse herself. Yet something was different about Jazzy's story: her father and grandfather were preachers. No one believed her when she told what they had done to her. And when she started sexually acting out at church and school, the family said the "devil" literally made her do it. She was possessed, they said, and asked for her to be removed from their home. Human Services was ready to remove her when the family, not wanting a major investigation, had her removed.

The deeply disturbing part of her story was not her acting out sexually, which was bad enough. She had to be watched carefully when boys were around. What disturbed most of us about her were ... well ... her "night terrors."

I sat drinking a cup of coffee when Janice came running into my office, out of breath.

"It's Jazzy again," she said.

"Did you take her to the 'Quiet Room?" I asked.

"Sure did. This one is bad ... really bad. You better come and see for yourself," she said excitedly.

"Okay, give me a minute to finish my coffee," I replied.

What could I do, I thought? The child was heavily medicated at night to avoid sleep problems. So much medication, in fact, that she had trouble getting awake in the mornings. She saw a therapist two times a week and the psychiatrist every two weeks. Still she had night terrors four or five nights a week. They would last several hours or all night till 4 or 5 in the morning. Then out of sheer exhaustion, she would fall asleep, on the floor of the quiet room.

I took one last sip of coffee and went out the door. Darn, would I ever get to finish a fresh cup of coffee on this job? I knew better.

Three staff workers were standing at the quiet room door, each taking a turn looking in the small window. They all seemed in awe of what they saw and heard. Two were new to this shift, and they had a rude awakening coming. You saw and heard things at night in a place like this you only thought happened in movies.

"Okay, how long has she been in there?" I asked.

Janice answered, "About 30 minutes."

"Are all other girls in her room asleep?" I queried.

"I think so," answered one of the new staff.

"Think so? Better be a yes. Please go check the room," I said sternly.

"She is really acting out tonight. It is wild," Janice said.

I approached the window and peered in. There was Jazzy doing her strange contortions. "Contortions," when described, lost something in the translation from the eye to the written word. Maybe it was the energy that surrounded Jazzy when she acted out. I'm not sure.

The air was very heavy and ominous when she was in one of these episodes. When she went into one of these terrors, a strange feeling of doom, or pervasive evil, seemed to lurk in every dark shadow of the hallway or room she was in.

Then the sounds began … strange, inhuman sounds. Not words or real parts of words. Real guttural sounds, like something in the wind on a late winter night. Sounds like moans … only they weren't quite moans. It was almost like something you hear in the woods … echoing and always out of sight; the sound of a mother animal grieving over one of her dying brood. Yes, it was almost like the death wail of a primitive people. Whatever they were, they were unnatural and eerie.

Many of the staff who worked at night with Jazzy had come to believe she might really be possessed.

"Melissa, I'm going in with her," I told the new
staff member assigned to Jazzy that night.

"Are you sure? I mean, is it safe? I mean…," she stopped.

"I don't know how safe it is, but if you and Janice keep
watch, and I get into trouble, come in quickly … and I
mean quickly. This girl is bigger than I am, and when she is
agitated, she's much stronger than any of us," I replied.

"Yes, ma'am. We'll keep a close watch,"
she said, her eyes big as saucers.

I opened the door to the quiet room and entered slowly.
Jazzy was in the back of the room banging her fists on
the padded wall and making all kinds of strange noises.
Squeaks, shrieks, and guttural clicking sounds came from
her body. She didn't turn around. I stood and watched.

Next she tried to seduce the wall, it seemed. Stroking it
with her hands gently and then raising her legs one at a
time, rubbing them against the wall. The motions were very
provocative and almost sensual. She was also rubbing her cheek
against the wall. What was this child doing, I thought?

I leaned against the door with no knob on the inside. It
could only be opened by someone on the outside … on
the other side. What kind of reality was I encountering
with this child inside this small padded room?

She turned around suddenly and leaped into a strange stance.
Her eyes fixed on me. I quickly stood straight and made direct
eye contact. It seemed like she was looking through me. Her
body was rigid as she stood there. Then she started swinging
her arms … not at me, just wildly swinging in all directions.

"Jasmine," I said, as I tried to bring her back to this reality.

She started twirling like a top in the middle of the room. Then she stopped and dropped to the floor on her knee. Guttural noises gurgled from her throat ... noises that were low in pitch and unearthly sounding. Her head swayed to the right and then the left.

I really didn't know what to do.

Jazzy began to tear around the room like an animal. She was bent over and kept hitting the walls.

"Jasmine, honey, it's Miss Pam. You need to go to bed. It is very late," I said, trying to get her attention in this world.

"NO," a deep voice answered.

I was startled. The voice didn't sound like Jasmine's.

"Get out of here," she continued.

"Jazzy," I pleaded.

"I SAID GET OUT!" the deep voice came out of her again.

What was going on inside this child? She stood up now and faced me. The look on her face was far from childish. This was not a game. This wasn't the 11-year-old Jazzy I knew.

"No ... I'm not leaving until you come with me to bed," I said with a slight tremor in my voice.

I didn't know how I would do what I said. But I was going to give it a try.

She glared at me. Then spit on the floor. At least it wasn't on me.

"NO … I don't want to. I don't want to go with you,"
she said, as her voice seemed to be talking now.

Schizophrenic? No, she hadn't been diagnosed as that, but
she was too young for such a label, anyway. Possessed? Well,
I was wondering. This was just too bizarre … an 11-year-old
girl talking in the voice of an old man? Acting, acting like
someone or something had control over her consciousness.

"I don't think so," I replied. "You are going
to come with me and go to bed."

After I spoke, she collapsed on the floor like a rag doll. More
demonic noises came from her mouth…. Her head began
jerking up and down. I reached out to touch her shoulder.

"Jazzy," I said, thinking a physical touch might break
the trance-like state she seemed to be in.

My hand glanced across her shoulder as she growled at me and
then went into a corner. There she crouched down like a cornered
animal and made those noises … unearthly, deep, and haunting.

I was stumped. What should I do? What could I do with a child
that would not talk or respond to any type of human outreach?

I had a feeling deep in my soul, a feeling like this child
might be beyond anything I could think of doing.
It was then that Janice came into the room. She was
carrying a boom box. Great idea, I thought.

She placed it on the floor next to me and then quickly left the
room. We usually didn't allow any objects in the quiet room.
This might work though. It was worth a try and the risk.

I bent down and pressed the "on" switch. Janice had placed a
cassette in the tape deck. Music began blasting out of the speakers.

I caught myself from nervously laughing when I heard the music.
It was Barbra Streisand. Must have been a staff tape, I thought.

The music filled the small room…. It was the song, "People."
Her eyes big as softballs, Jazzy glared at the boom box. I
thought, oh, no…. Then she put her hands over her ears and
started a kind of howling. It sounded more like a painful
cry or moan, unlike any I had or have ever heard.

I turned up the music, and she cried out with a louder noise.

"Wonderful music, huh, Jazzy?" I yelled over the music.

She kept her hands over her ears and started shaking
her head back and forth. Her braids were swinging
wildly, as she began kicking the walls with her feet.

"Oh, you like the music?" I asked.

She continued to kick and then scream, "NO! NO!" she said in
her own voice, or at least it began to sound like her own voice.

"I love music," I said loudly over her screaming garbled words.

"No! Turn it off!" she yelled at me.

"Why? You like music, Jazzy. I see you dancing all
the time around the other girls," I replied.

I turned the volume down a few levels. Jazzy kept kicking
and holding her hands to her ears. Then she finally fell to
the floor. The song faded out and I stopped the music. Jazzy
was piled on the floor, her hands still over her ears. Now the
sounds coming from deep within her were wailing sobs.

"Jazzy," I said kneeling down and touching her should gently.
"Jazzy. It's time to go to bed, honey. You must be tired."

Her sobs continued and her body trembled. Now I embraced her shaking body, trying to absorb some of the pain pouring from her soul. After what seemed like forever, I could feel the trembling begin to ease, and she began to nestle in my arms. The sobs gave way to baby-like moans. Her hands came away from her ears, and she stuck her right thumb in her mouth. I rocked her slowly, and softly sang a lullaby my grandmother and mother used to sing when my brothers and I were little.

"Bye-o ... bye-o ... bye-o ... bye," I sang
almost as a whisper in her ear.

There we sat until Jazzy fell asleep, either from sheer exhaustion or the soothing whisper of an old Welsh lullaby. Several hours went by and finally morning came. A staff member entered the room, and we picked up Jazzy and moved her to her bed. The other children were off to school, and we let Jazzy sleep, for the demons inside her had been vanquished for awhile, until the next outburst, which was assuredly around the corner.

I went back to my office, physically and emotionally spent and fell onto the old couch. Tired beyond my limits, I couldn't turn off my mind. What was buried so deep in this child? Was there such a thing as demonic possession?

Moments like these made any rational person question all the psychology and science that modern wisdom offered to explain. Definitely no textbook theories or techniques worked, no medicine ever stopped the dramatic episodes, unless she was completely sedated.

Finally, my mind gave way to sleep.

Two weeks after this episode, Jazzy was transferred to a psychiatric hospital. She didn't go willingly. Sedatives

were administered; she was wrapped up in a sterile white
sheet and carried to the van that transported her away.

I never got a chance to say good-bye. None of the staff did.
The decision was made by the doctor of the home in one of
those closed-off staff meetings, where only psychiatrists, the
director of counseling, and the home director were present.

The Jazzy file final entry said only: "child transferred to a
secure medical center for she posed a threat to herself and
others." A convenient way to pass on the problem child on
to another program — another group of childcare providers
who were foreign and alien to this child and her issues.

 Many children like Jazzy get moved around through a system
ill prepared to deal with problems as traumatic as hers, I thought
on the morning I arrived at work and found her gone. Listening
to one of my staff report the scene of her transfer was painful.
My mind ran over the many nights spent confronting her
demons with her. Never winning the battle but always being
beside her in those moments of awesome pain and chilling dread
that pervaded the quiet room when Jazzy became overcome
by some power imbedded deep within her young body.

What was Jazzy saying to me? To the staff? To the
doctors? To the therapists? To anyone who would listen? I
believe she was saying, "Help me ... please, help me!"

Many will think this is not a proper psychological assessment
or medical diagnosis, but remember the only things capable
of entering her moments of extreme rage and convulsive
actions that had any effect were music and human touch.

Sedatives just masked the problem. Regular medication never
stopped the episodes from happening, and intensive therapeutic
counseling never saw this part of Jazzy. The deep hurt, the dark
trauma, the "demons" in her soul could only be touched and

affected by love. Jazzy's love of music, or the love of another human being was the only thing that could help confront the pain. We miss it ... all the time. We are not listening to the children.

Again, another damaged child slipped through the system....

Peter's Story

"When we acknowledge a child's feelings, we do him a great service. We put him in touch with his inner reality. And once he's clear about that reality, he gathers the strength to begin to cope." - Adele Faber

When I went to work for the Human Services Department, I was enthusiastic, full of energy and had innovative ideas about helping children caught in crisis. Did I learn how naïve I was? Yes. Very quickly.

Peter was a quiet, withdrawn little boy. When we first met, his clothes were dingy and too small even for his frail, boney frame. His dark burnt red hair was cut with cowlicks popping out of his head, as if someone had purposely cut his hair uneven. (I would later learn that his mother cut his hair because he couldn't sit still long enough for any barber.)

He wore the usual clothing for a nine year old: blue jeans, a short-sleeved pullover striped shirt, sneakers with worn-out soles and dirty white socks that needed to be bleached white again.

He was a child of few words, and he never looked up when he spoke. His greenish brown eyes seemed to be focused on those dirty worn sneakers. Peter's vocabulary the first few weeks I worked with him consisted of "nope," "yup," "I dunno" and "maybe." And what really bothered me about Peter --- he never smiled or laughed.

The psychiatrist that Peter was seeing said he was ADD and clinically depressed. So he was on Ritalin and Mellaril:

Ritalin three times a day and Mellaril two times a day. Pretty hefty doses of drugs for a nine year old! His problem? Well, if Peter didn't stay on the drugs, he would act out in school and at home, not follow directions, wander away from the classroom or go sit in the bathroom alone. Sometimes, he would just be oppositional and defiant to any authority figure.

So what was Peter's story? The case record reported that when Peter was 4 years old, he had to watch his baby brother burn to death in a boating accident. He jumped off the boat to safety and watched his brother die while his mother supposedly ran for help. The report pointedly stated that Peter never appeared to show any feelings about the incident. He never talked about it or ever cried. He had extensive therapy and counseling since then. The consensus of the therapists stated that Peter had repressed anger issues … all agreed these were directed toward his mother. There was no mention of his father included anywhere in the case.

The only positive points in the case report stated that Peter's I.Q. was above normal — when he cooperated long enough for any testing. Yet, his school grades were all failing, and he never finished any assignments his teachers gave him.

Peter lived with his mother and stepfather (mother's long-time live-in) way out in the country on a non-working farm. They had lots of animals: horses, chickens and goats. One of Peter's chores — one of many for a nine year old — was to feed the chickens and goats. This seemed to be a point of importance for Peter, and he did this task daily with no problem. In fact, he would disappear for hours sometimes (so his mother reported) when he went to feed the animals.

When I went to do my first home visit, the animals were what Peter wanted to show me first. My visit to his home and room was a short "this is it" — "and now here are the goats and the horses." One interesting observation I made on that first visit to his home was that I saw no toys in his room and not any anywhere around the house. The house was very messy and in need of much repair. His mother was a waitress at a local café, and the stepfather was a pseudo mechanical handyman, who worked when someone had a job for him. Money was tight in this household, and Peter knew it.

It was a rainy, dark morning in May when I first met Peter. I went to his school to observe behavior problems the teacher was having with him. After checking in with the school office, I was directed to go down several hallways. The school year was almost at an end, and as I passed noisy classrooms with children eager to get out of this place for summer break, my eyes caught sight of a little boy standing with his nose up against a corridor corner. I knew it was him … "the goat boy," as his case report had said his classmates called him.

I walked up to him…. "Peter?" I said with a question in my voice.

He didn't look away from the wall.

"Hi, I'm Miss Pam," I said reaching out to touch his shoulder with my hand. He flinched as I touched him, but never turned an eye in my direction

"Peter, I am here to talk with you. Your teacher said you have been having some problems and you might need someone to talk to," I said as I drew my hand away. I then squatted next to him, my back against the dingy grey cinderblock wall. He didn't move or speak. I continued to try and break the strain in our first encounter.

"I work with lots of kids who have problems in school and at home. We talk about the problems and figure out ways to help the problems go away. Sometimes we go to the park or to the creek or other places … and just play and laugh and talk. Do you like to go to the park?" I asked, praying he would respond and that I had found a "button."

He moved his head slightly toward me. His eyes glanced at me and then back at the wall. Then he spoke, "I never been to a park."

"Really? Well, we'll have to go there then. Would you like to take a walk with me?" I asked.

"Can't," he answered very quietly.

"Yes, you can. I am here to take you for a walk," I answered back. I didn't wait for a reply; I stood and took hold of his hand.

"Come on, let's go outside for a walk," I said.

Peter let me take his hand, and he turned toward me, his head still bent down and his eyes focused on his feet.

"I won't get in trouble?" he asked.

"No, you won't get in trouble. Your teacher and the principal know I am here to see you. Let's go outside," I said.

We walked down the hallway until we came to the double doors leading outside to the parking lot. Peter let me keep hold of his hand and walked beside me with no resistance. He kept his head bent down, never looking my way or any way except down.

I pushed the bar that opened the door, and out into the dark breezy late morning day we went. It felt like rain might spoil our walk at any moment. We proceeded across the paved parking lot to the field beside the school. The grass was over our ankles, and the breeze kept warning it was blowing in a storm. Out in this area, summer storms blew in off the lakes quickly and could be filled with electrical activity — lightning that was spectacular but deadly in the same moment. I tried to keep one eye on the sky and one on this sad little boy walking next to me, his hand still in mine.

"Feels like it might rain," I said.

"Yup," he replied. I was surprised he spoke,
and it caught me a little off guard.

"Do you like rain storms?" I asked. Another leading
question might provoke a conversation, I thought.

"Yup," he replied, his eyes never looking up.

We kept walking through the field. This was a child
either far removed from his feelings or from reality itself,
I thought as we walked on. I didn't push him to talk.
Something told me just the presence of walking and that
he kept his hand in mine was enough for this moment.

Finally, we came to a wire fence.

"Guess we have to go back now. We've run out of field," I said.

"Yup," he replied.

We turned around and stared back toward the school building.
The dark clouds were building, making the sky ominous looking
and the breeze was now gusty. I picked up the pace of our walk,
knowing it was going to pour on us any moment. Peter's short
legs kept pace with mine, even though I wasn't that much taller
than he was. When the thunder started, his hand squeezed mine.
Now I was not holding his hand, he was holding mine. When
the second clap of thunder sounded, he looked up for the first
time. A bolt of lightning glanced across the horizon to the west.

"We better hurry," he said.

"Yup," I answered.

So we walked quickly back to the school building. I took Peter
directly to his classroom and deposited him with his teacher.

Before leaving, I turned to him and said, "I will see you next Thursday after school, and we'll go to the park." He looked me in the eyes, let go of my hand, walked sullenly to his desk and sat down. The teacher and I smiled at each other, and I left.

Peter was delivered to my office by his mother. He walked in with his head down. He had on another striped t-shirt, blue jeans and his dirty sneakers.

"Hi," I said, as he rounded my desk and stood in front of me. His hand reached out and touched my arm.

"Want to go to the park?" I asked. He nodded his head, never looking up. "Okay, then, off to the park we go," I said as I took hold of his dirty little hand. His sun-tanned arms and hands looked like he hadn't bathed in weeks. He was dark not just from the sun but also from layers of dirt and sweat.

"Here we go," I said. Then out the door we went to my car.

The short journey to the park was only a mile or so. We rode in silence with Peter never looking my way or out the windows of the car. It was a beautiful sunny day with white billowy clouds crisscrossing the afternoon sky. The park entrance was before us in minutes.

"Well, have you ever been here before?" I asked, trying to break the silence. He shook his head no, not even trying to sneak a peak at the park. I turned the car into the park and pulled into a parking space.

"Let's go. This will be fun," I said. I opened my door and got out. Peter just sat in the car seat staring at his feet. I walked to his side of the car and opened the door.

"Come on, let's go swing," I said, as I took hold
of his arm and moved out of the car. Slowly, he
shuffled along side of me toward the swings.

"Here, you take this one, and I'll take the one next to it," I said.
Peter sat on the swing, his arms limp by his side. I began to pump
my legs and make the swing rise into the air. He just sat there,
head bent down to the ground and his eyes fixed upon his shoes.

"Hey, Peter, see how high you can go," I challenged
him. He sat there like a log on the swing.

I stopped pumping my swing and dragged my feet to stop.
Then I got off my swing and walked behind his. I took hold
of his hands and placed them around the swing's chains.
He grasped the chains and I pushed him. Now he had
to look up — the ground wasn't there anymore. I pushed
and pushed, and he rose higher into the sky. Suddenly, he
started pumping his legs. I stood back from the swing.

The sullen little boy was swinging on his own, pushing
out with his legs and then pulling back on the swing with
his arms. His eyes were now focused above his head.

"All right, Peter!" I yelled, encouraging him to keep going. I
went back to my swing and began to pump and rise again.

"It's fun, isn't it?" I queried.

"Yup," he said.

His head was bent back, and he seemed to be swinging for
the sun. I don't know how long we were on those swings … a
long time, I think, because my legs were ready to start having
muscle cramps when Peter's swing began to slow down.

Once his swing came to a stop, he jumped off and ran behind me.

"Let me push," he said as he began to push my back.

"Okay," I said. He pushed and pushed me, allowing my legs to rest.

It was getting late, and I knew over an hour had passed, and I had to get him back to my office. His mother would be waiting. Somehow I knew she wasn't the type of person who liked to wait.

"I think we better stop now, Peter. We have to go back to my office; your mother will be waiting for you," I told him.

"No!" he sharply replied.

I was surprised by his response. This little guy was a person of few words, but when he did say something, his tone said more than his words.

"Sorry, kiddo, but it is time to stop playing and go," I replied as I dragged my feet in the dirt to stop the swing.

"NO!" he said back to me. "I don't want to go home."

I jumped out of the swing and turned to face him. He was looking at the ground or his feet, whichever, again.

"Sorry, my friend, it's time to go," I said reaching for his hand. I took hold of his hand and slowly pulled him toward the car. When we got to the passenger door, I let go of his hand. He stood there sullenly.

Wow, I thought, as I walked around the car to get to my side. This is one angry child. What is going on inside his mind, I wondered? I got in the car, and we went back to my office in silence again.

When we drove up to the building, his mother was
standing outside by her car. Peter never looked as I
approached the building and stopped. I turned off the
car and got out. His mother seemed a little agitated.

"I've been waiting about 15 minutes," she said
to me in an annoyed tone of voice.

"Sorry, we just lost track of time. We were having so
much fun...," I didn't get to finish my sentence.

"Fun?! Peter doesn't know how to have fun," she said as she
walked over to the car, opened the door, reached for his
arm and yanked him out of the seat. "Peter has no friends.
Peter doesn't play with other kids. Peter doesn't do much
of anything," she said as she pulled him toward the car.

"I have to hurry, or I'll be late for work," she said as she was
pushing Peter into the car. "Maybe you should pick him
up for these meetings and bring him home after. It would
make it a lot easier on me," she said matter-of-factly.

"Well, that might be a possibility," I replied.

"Good, let's get it set up that way from now on. I just don't
have time for all this toting him around," she said.

She got in her car, started it and left. The image of Peter
that day still lingers often in my mind. As she tore out of the
parking lot, he glanced my way. His sad eyes moved and caught
mine for a brief instant ... his head still bent down ... he had
dared to glance my way. He had SEEN me for a moment.

I drove to Peter's house and picked him up for our
next "session." Today was going to be an event to be
remembered — a visit to Wal-Mart's Toy Department.

Peter was waiting at the end of his driveway, which was a dirt road. I was glad I didn't have to traverse it since it was full of deep holes and protruding boulders. Traveling up the road to the house was an adventure in defensive driving and avoiding a sharp edge from one of the rocks, which could easily cause a flat tire.

As I pulled up, he was kicking stones into a pothole deep enough to hold water up to your knees. Peter saw my car out of a corner eye glance. He stopped kicking the stones and sauntered slowly toward my car. It appeared as if he were wearing the same dingy clothes I always saw him in. I stopped the car and got out.

"Hey, Peter, ready to go on another adventure?" I asked smiling.

"Yup," he replied, as he came to the passenger door. This time he opened the car door himself and got in. I turned the car around and we went off to "Wally-World."

"How have you been this week?" I asked.

"Okay," he answered. His head was bent down as usual and, of course, he was silent.

"We are going to have a great adventure today," I said enthusiastically, trying to peak his curiosity.

He didn't respond. Peter just sat there looking down at his feet. The trip was about 20 minutes from his farm, and the silence was … well, I decided we would have music instead of silence, so I turned on the radio. The oldies station I usually listened to came on, and I began to sing along. Peter rode in silence.

Finally, the mall sign appeared around the curve. We were at our destination, "Wally-World," as the locals called it. I pulled into the parking lot.

"Here we are," I said.

He looked up. "Wally-World," he said. Amazing, I thought, something caught his attention.

"Do you like coming here?" I asked.

"Yup," he said, turning his head toward the store.

"Does your mom bring you here?" I asked.

"Yup."

"What do you buy when you come?" I asked, trying to keep the conversation going.

"Nothin'."

"Nothin'? Oh, I'll bet you get clothes here, and toys … and," he interrupted me.

"Nope, nothin'," he said. "I just look … she buys clothes for her," he said.

"How about toys?" I asked, now that he was volunteering information.

"Nope," he said very bluntly.

"Well, today we are going to the toy department," I said, thinking this would peak his interest.

"Okay," he replied.

I parked the car, and we hopped out quickly. This time he came around to me and took my hand as we walked across the parking lot to the store. His strides were quicker and his head,

although bent, kept lifting up sneaking glances at the store.
We entered the electronic doorway and went off to toy land.

We walked up and down aisles. His head was no longer bent down
to the ground. Peter was looking and checking out the overstocked
shelves with toys barely hanging on to the edges of the shelves.

This was a remarkable day … a moment my heart and mind
will never forget. Peter walked up and down the toy aisles
making noises I cannot describe. They were oohhhs and
ahhhs of delight. He uttered little sighs of awe and wonder.
After a few minutes, he began to talk, really talk.

"These are really cool. Look!" he said, as he pointed
to a Star Wars vehicle. He touched the toys carefully
and put his nose to many and eyeballed others.

"I never seen so many toys," he said as he
went up and down the toy lanes.

I stood and watched this little boy in amazement. It was
as if he had never been in a toy department before. He
was overwhelmed and he was showing emotions.

"Peter, have you ever been in this part of
Wal-Mart before?" I asked.

"No! Never," he said as he continued exploring the toys.

I couldn't believe his answer. Never been in the
Wal-Mart toy department? That couldn't be. But
watching him react as he was, I believed him.

We spent over an hour just eyeballing, touching, and just
checking out all the wonderful playthings most children take
for granted. He was amazed. He never asked to buy anything.
Peter was content just to be among the shelves and look.

"Wow," slipped out of the mouth. "Cool." All the usual kid expressions began to roll out of the child.

When he would find something that really caught his interest, he would call me to come and look. He would show me, and then place it back on the shelf where he found it. Finally, it was time to leave. I hated to break the spell these toys had over him, but it was time to return him to reality — his home.

"It's time to go, Peter," I said, reaching for his hand.

"Oh," he said with sadness in his voice.

He didn't resist or throw a tantrum. Slowly, we walked away from the walls of toys and back to the car. He opened his own door and jumped in.

"Can we come back sometime?" he asked, looking at me.

"Sure," I said, smiling.

The ride back to his house was silent, although Peter raised his head and looked out the windows this time. He even glanced toward me at moments. When we approached his driveway, his mood changed, and he bent his head down again. I stopped the car at the gate. He opened the door and slid out.

He went to slam the door, but then he stopped and peeked his head inside again.

"Thanks, I really liked that," he almost smiled when he spoke. Then he shut the door gently and started up the rugged pot-holed driveway.

As I drove away, I watched him slowly climb the road to his house out of my rearview mirror. Hands in his jeans pockets and head bent down, he kicked stones as he meandered home.

My next visit was at his home. It was a late July afternoon, and it was one of those steamy, hot days. I drove the hazardous driveway to his house, carefully avoiding the potholes and huge rocks. The road could easily tear out the bottom of any car.

I saw Peter standing by a shed as I parked the car and got out.

"Hi!" I yelled as I waved to him.

He looked up and almost smiled. I looked around the area and saw no other vehicles or people.

"Hey, is your mom or dad home?" I asked.

"Nope," he answered.

"Oh, where are they?"

"Workin'."

"Okay, what do you want to do today?" I asked.

He looked up at me with those sad eyes, and they came alive.

"Ya wanna see my animals? I gotta feed 'em," he said.

"Sure, sounds like fun," I answered.

We went into one of the sheds and Peter got a bucket. Then he went over to a big wooden bin, opened the lit and scooped out some awful smelling feed. He filled the bucket brim full.

"Come on. I feed the horses first."

I walked beside him, wanting to offer to carry the bucket since it pulled his small body over to one side. We started walking down a narrow dirt path toward a small pond. We came to a barbed wire fence, and Peter let out a shrill whistle. I heard a sound and then saw the two horses come up over a small hill. A beautiful Palomino and a small Paint pony came running toward Peter. He ducked under the rusty wire fence.

"You comin'?" he asked without hesitation.

I surveyed the fence and figured I could hold a wire up and pass through, hopefully not catching a barb on my clothes. The strange horses were another issue. I was raised around all kinds of horses, but these looked range wild. What the heck, I thought; I could always run. So I lifted the wire and went into the pasture with Peter.

He walked out to the galloping horses, sat the bucket down in front of him and then made some strange "horse-type" noises. The horses came and stopped in front of him. They didn't go for the bucket of feed; instead, they started making horse noises at Peter. He reached to touch them and they bent their heads into his body. I watched them play.

This sad, sullen boy took on a different aura. The horses pushed at him with their noses, and he pushed and stroked them. A smile — yes, a real smile — came over his face! He took feed from the bucket in his hands, and the horses ate while he talked with them. I couldn't hear what he was saying. Whatever it was, every now and then one of the horses would nudge Peter playfully. It was quite a sight to watch.

Finally, the feed was gone and the bucket was empty. He looked toward me and motioned for me to come closer. I walked over to him.

"This is Halo," he said pointing to the Palomino.
"And this is Windstar," he said as he playfully
pushed the neck of the smaller Paint pony.

"Hi, Halo, hi Windstar," I said, reaching to touch them. Both
horses shied away from me. Peter made a sound from deep in
his throat and horses stood still. The boy took my hand and
placed it on Halo's neck. The horse eyed me but stood still. Then
Peter moved my hand to Windstar's nose and I rubbed it.

"They don't like strangers much," he said.
"They don't really like people much."

"Oh," I said, continuing to rub the Paint's nose.

"They don't see many people…. They like me though," he said.

"Do you ride them, Peter?" I asked.

"Ah … Halo lets me get on her back sometimes. They
don't like no saddles. They don't like people much. They
like to run wild," he said. "Somebody hurt Halo before
she came here. She used to be mean and kick and bite.
I made her learn. I made her be nice," he said.

"How did you do that, Peter?"

"Well, I just spend a lot of time with her
and talk to her and touch her nice."

"Oh, I see…. Do you think someone was mean to her?" I queried.

"Yeah, and nobody spent time talking to her," he replied

Suddenly Peter picked up the bucket. Some thought came
into his mind that seemed to change his whole persona.

"We gotta go feed the goats. They get hungry and there's lots of 'em. Come on," he was taking control and we were moving on.

We left the horses and climbed back through the barbed wire fence. Back to the rundown shed we walked. Peter threw the bucket against the wall. He picked up a cloth sack full of some kind of feed and put it on his back.

"Okay, it's the goats' time," he said.

"Okay, lead the way," I answered.

We walked down another dirt trail. This one was wider than the horse pasture one. I felt now was the time to try and probe Peter, get him to open up more. He seemed to be in his comfort zone here among the animals.

"Peter, do you like school?" I asked lightly.

"Sometimes," he replied.

"What is your favorite thing to do in school?"

"Listen to stories," he said with no hesitation.

"Oh, do you like to read?" There was a pause now in the conversation. Peter got a frown line across his forehead.

"I like to see the pictures," was his guarded reply. There was a long silence. "I better like to listen to the stories" he said, finally breaking the heaviness of the moment.

What was he telling me, I wondered? He didn't like to read out loud in class, maybe? Perhaps he liked to hear the teacher animate a story? Then I thought. maybe Peter couldn't read! No one had said anything about that. Could that be why he didn't do any schoolwork? What was Peter telling me? My mind was wandering over all these thoughts when Peter let out a blood-curdling scream.

Peter began running with all his might down the path. I started chasing him. He rounded a corner, and as I caught up with him, I found him bent over what looked like a baby goat. I stopped running. I stopped dead still on the path and watched Peter. I could see the little goat was lifeless. Peter was stroking its neck and talking to it. This time, I was close enough to hear what Peter was saying.

"It's okay, little baby. It's okay now. I'm here ... I'll make you okay. I will find your mama. She will come and help you ... she won't leave you," he said with no tears or quiver in his voice.

I bent down to the goat. It had blood on its neck, and there was a pool of blood under its body. There appeared to be no life in the little creature. Peter took its bloody head and neck in his arms and kept talking.

"It will be okay.... I will find your mama and she will make you okay," he kept saying over and over.

I let Peter go on for about 15 minutes. Then I bent down to the boy and the goat. What do you tell a child about death? Especially a child who has had a traumatic encounter with death? My mind was racing. How do I keep Peter in the reality of the moment? All these kinds of thoughts were spinning in my mind, when Peter stood up with the little goat in his arms.

"I gotta take him to his mama," he said matter-of-factly. "He ain't gonna be okay and I can't help him."

"Peter...," I tried to interject.

"The little baby's gone to God now. I know, just like my little brother. But his mama's gotta say good-bye ...

she can't just run away," he said as he carried the little
goat toward the herd of goats out in the field.

I stood there frozen, watching the little boy carry the little
goat through the tall grass toward the herd. The goats didn't
scatter; they let him enter their midst. He appeared to be
looking for one goat in particular. Finally, he found her — the
mother goat. He laid the baby goat down next to her and sat
beside them. The mother goat began to blat out goat noises.
She lowered her head and smelled the little goat; then, she
smelled the boy now covered with goat blood. She licked some
of the blood from the lifeless little goat and turned away.

Peter picked up the baby goat and walked back toward me as
the goats separated, leaving him a pathway to get through.
There were perhaps 100 of them all bunched together.
Slowly, up the field he walked until he was at my side.

"I gotta bury the baby now," he said, still without tears.

"Let me help you, Peter," I said.

"Nope, this is my job," he said. "My dad will
make me do it later, I wanna do it now."

"Okay.... Can I come with you?" I asked quietly.

"Nope. Somebody's gotta feed the goats. You can do that," he said.

"Okay. How do I feed them?" I asked.

"Take that bag of feed and spread it out at the
corners of the field around those goats. You know,
kinda like piles in the four corners. Okay?"

"Okay," I said, although I had never fed goats before.

Peter headed up the path toward the barns, carrying the dead
baby goat, his head bent down to the ground as he walked.

After feeding the goats I went to look for Peter. I found
him down behind one of the barns placing rocks on top
of a dirt pile, where I assumed he buried the baby goat.
When he finished placing the last rock he laid down on the
ground next to the grave. When more than fifteen minutes
had passed I walked down the small ridge toward him.

As I approached he turned his head toward me
and I could see his eyes were wet with tears. I
stopped and sat down a few feet from him.

"Are you okay Peter?" I said quietly, as the wind
blew my words out into the pasture.

"I wish I could have saved him," he replied as the tears
rolled down his face. "He was just a baby an
I….."

"Death comes sometimes when we don't expect it, Peter,
and we can not do anything about it." I replied.

"Yea….I know."

He continued to cry and now he pounded the ground with his fist.

"I can't save anybody….not even a baby goat. They are
my animals to take care an' I'm gonna be in trouble
when my Dad finds out." He said as he now kicked the
ground with his feet and pounded with his fist.

"This is not your fault. It was the goats time to die,
Peter. Even his mother couldn't save him."

"Why……..Why? He was just a baby!"

His kicking and fist pounding stopped and he rolled over facing me. He rubbed the tears away with his now dirt covered hands.

"I don't know why Peter….only God knows why," I said as I bent down toward him. A very inadequate answer I thought, but again another of those "God moments" where I said a quick prayer and hoped my words were correct for the moment.

"I let my baby die too." He buried his face in the ground and rolled onto his stomach again.

A silence seemed to come into the air on the ridge. I watched the young boy continue to cry not knowing if I should reach out and try to sooth his pain with human touch or just sit quietly by his side and let just my presence be of some comfort.

Peter broke the painful moment.

"I had a baby brother once…….and he died. She didn't help him and I din't help….He burned up."

Help me God, I thought what do I say? What do I do for this boy?

"Peter that was a really awful thing to happen.I am sorry you had to see that, but you were very little then and it was not your fault what happened," I stumbled over my words as I spoke carefully.

"I remember him cryin' and screamin'. My mom she just ran and left us there," he said continuing to cry with his hands covering his face. "At least the baby goat didn't burn….my baby burned."

Now I reached for the dirty little "goat boy" and his limp body rolled into my arms. His sobbing continued as I held him and ran my fingers though his hair. I held him and the wind blew across the ridge carrying his pain and his fear and his anger with it.

After awhile his sobbing stopped, and his eyes opened
wide. He looked up at the sky and sighed.

"I'm sorry I couldn't save the baby goat, Miss Pam.
An I'm sorry my baby brother burned and died. I
wish I could have saved them both," he said.

"I know you wish you could have saved both of
them. I wish that could have been too." I replied
looking into his dirty face smeared with tears.

"They will tell me this is my fault....the baby goat dyin',
just like my brother. He will punish me...jus'
like God."

"Who will punish you Peter?"

"My dad. He says all the time I can't do nothin' right, that's why
the goats are mine to take care of and prove I can do it right."

"Peter, you do a great job with the animals and they
love you. This baby goat didn't die because of you."

"They will think so....an I will be punished.
You'll see....you'll see," he said fearfully.

"I will talk with your parents Peter. The death of the baby goat is
not your fault.........and the death of your baby brother was not
your fault. That was an accident." I said trying to calm his fears.

"I'm pretty angry at God, you know. And I really know
nobody here wants me around. She says I remind her
every day about my brother and it makes her sad. If he
was still alive things would be different....my mom tells
me that all the time. Maybe I should just die."

How do I answer that? What do I say?
Please God help me one more time.

"Peter, you have to let go of the anger. God doesn't want you
to be angry all the time. And dying won't bring back your
brother or the baby goat. You have to live to take care of
all the other animals that depend on you and love you."

"Why, Miss Pam? Why?" his voice was pleading.

"Because God gave you a special gift Peter…a gift
of loving and caring for animals. Someday your mom and
dad will see that. You are alive and you are a blessing for
all these animals who you care for. And that is a good
thing," I said sitting him up and looking at him directly.

"I love all the animals, Miss Pam. I really do. They are my
friends and they are sorta my family. Like brothers and
sisters," he said with energy coming back to his voice.

"Yes, Peter, they are like your family, and they do
love you because you love and care for them."

He stood up and the wind blew his hair back around
his eyes. The tears were gone and his eyes searched
around the fields checking out his animals, from his horses to
the chickens to the goats; they were all there waiting for him.

I stood up and we walked hand in hand up the ridge.
Peter's healing time was beginning and the release
of those lonely tears for the baby goat were tears for a
baby brother he couldn't save. But maybe the baby goat's
death was a turning point that would save Peter.

DERRICK'S STORY

"Children also need opportunities to practice being less than perfect. They can afford to be ill-tempered with us because it is our love that is most constant. Steadfast love provides a safe haven." - *Cathy Rindner Tempelsman*

The day was brisk and windy. The sun poking out from behind wispy clouds made this early day in January seem more like April or May. I arrived at my office early to catch up on dreaded paperwork. Boring, redundant and detailed paperwork seems to be endless when you work in social services agencies.

I was the Program Director of a new pilot outreach program for runaway and homeless youth, where each day the piles on my desk grew taller. This day a young man arrived at my office who would greatly affect how I viewed runaway kids forever.

In a dirty black overcoat and with long rakish blonde hair hanging down on his shoulders, he entered the shelter main office. I caught a glimpse of him as he walked up to the receptionist.

Soon I would smell the brackish young man who entered the building. He took a seat after speaking with Connie and opened up a small black book. Appearing to be intently reading his little black book on his lap, his eyes darted around the room, checking out everyone and everything, I assumed. Everything of value, that is!

Several moments later, my phone rang. It was Connie.

"You have a visitor, Ms. U. Says he walked two miles
to get here to your office," she said softly.

"Really," I replied. "I guess if he would walk two miles,
I need to see him as soon as possible. I didn't really
want to do paperwork today…. Did I, Connie?"

She laughed quietly and said, "You never want to do paperwork."

"Right," I said back with no hesitation. The staff new me
well. Paperwork was always my last priority and that would
mean many all-night writing stints to catch up when reports
were due. "Connie, set up the small therapy room, and I will
see this young man in a few minutes. Thanks," I replied.

The therapy room had large soft chairs, and an unattractive,
green sofa and a coffee table with names carved into it.
Names of the many who had passed this way at some moment
of their young lives. Loud colorful prints of rock bands
adorned the rose-colored walls, and eight windows splashed
light throughout the comfy hardwood-floored room.

Yes, it was light and colorful but also open and comforting. Not
some depressing cubical with a desk, several chairs, fake plants
and a dreary faux masterpiece print on the wall. We don't seem
to understand that kids hate "four walls and two chairs with
a desk in between." They equate it with prison or punishment
of various kinds. Actually, I do not believe anyone likes to be
kept in "four walls" for very long. Plus, it is not conducive to
relaxing and creating trust when someone feels trapped in a
sterile room with one way in and one way out. Windows have
always seemed to create energy, warmth, light, depth and a
more inviting open feeling to any room. (That's why I use Dairy
Queens for therapy sessions with kids — lots of windows.)

I sat in one of the big oversized chairs and waited. Connie
brought the young man into the room within minutes

after I began to prepare the paperwork that would have
to be filled out with the boy to provide services.

He entered the room still wrapped in his big black overcoat
and very worn black work boots. He tossed his long fairly
long, unkempt hair over his shoulder and took a seat on the
green sofa across from me. When he sat down, he laid his
book on the coffee table and pushed the long bangs from
his face, which reached well below his chin. He tilted his
head and looked at me with a cocky crooked half smile.

"I'm Derrick," he said, his greenish eyes had a glint of mystery
caught by the rays of light coming through the windows.

What an interesting smile, I thought. His eyes were such
an unusual color that one would not quickly forget them.
The scar across his forehead ran to his right eyebrow. It was
deep but old. Must have been a painful injury a long time
ago that left such a mark on him. Yet the line gave character
to his young soft face framed by the dirty brackish hair.

"Hello, Derrick," I replied, as I stood and reached out my hand.
"I'm Ms. U, the Program Director of Shelter Outreach."

"Yeah, I heard about you … and the shelter. That's why I'm here,"
he said, still smiling. He reached out his hand to shake mine.

His hands were rough and his fingernails full of dirt, not an
inviting hand to touch, but we shook. It was the right thing to do.

"What's your book?" I asked, pointing to
his worn black book on the table.

"That," he reached for it and showed me as he continued, "is
what some street preacher gave me a couple weeks back. He
told me I better get saved, get right, or I would be on the streets
forever. I'd die on the streets some night, he said. I been readin'

it though," he stopped and threw the book on the table. Then he looked me straight in the eye. "Ma'am, I don't belong on the streets. I don't want to die on the streets. That's for sure. I haven't had a good meal in weeks … no, months. And I can't remember when I had a bath last," his head fell into his hands.

"Derrick," I quietly spoke his name. (There is power in a name. Do you realize how many times someone calls you or does not call you by name in just a 24-hour period?)

"Derrick," I spoke his name again.

He looked up with those green eyes through his filthy, long, stringy hair. "Ma'am, I believe in God, or I believe in a lot of what I been readin'. But I wasn't raised in a church, and I don't trust those people inside. You gotta be all dressed up to even get in the door. I sure can't smell like I smell and go in there. Yeah, that preacher guy brings me peanut butter sandwiches every noon down by the river place, but we gotta listen to his preachin' and a lot of it is about…. Oh, never mind. I'm here," he said as he sat up straight on the sofa and ran his crusty fingers through his hair.

"Yes, Derrick, you are here," I replied as I looked directly into his eyes. He wasn't high or drunk, though he reeked of cigarettes and dirt. "What kind of help do you need?"

"I'm homeless and I want to sleep in a real bed again. I want to eat real food, not some dumpster leftovers or 'road kill' the travelers are cookin' under the pipes," he said.

I saw real desperation in his eyes as he spoke.

"We can help you, Derrick. But we have rules here. This is not the street. How long have you been on the street?" I asked.

"A couple of months, most of the winter so far. I'm tired of sleepin' in boxes and over heat duct vents from the shops downtown. I can follow rules. You don't know me. This ain't my fault being here on the street. My mom kicked me out!" he said in a loud, angry voice.

"Really, I see. Why did your mom kick you out?"

"'Cause, 'cause I," he said his voice getting louder, as his head reared back and he threw his long hair back over the crown of his head.

Then he began to rub his head and bang his hand against the back of the sofa.

"I took Mom's car to go to a friend's house, and I had an accident. Drove into a ditch. I wasn't drinking or nothing, just going too fast! Mom and my step-dad showed up. She was furious, screaming and yelling at me. Never, not one time did she ask if I was okay! Nope, she was too upset about her car. It was totaled, my step-dad said. After they let me out of the hospital, I went home with my parents, and Mom packed one bag for me. Then she threw it out the door and told me to get out of her house and out of her life. She said she had enough of me. She said I had to pay for her car and I better get a job!" he stopped and stared out one of the windows.

"I see, quite a short story, but I am sure there is a long version, too! Let's get you settled into the emergency shelter and assess whether you qualify for the Transitional Living Program we have here. You game for that?" I asked.

He looked at me through the strands of dirty, greasy hair that covered most of his face when it fell straight down.

"Yeah. Can I get a bath, too?" Derrick asked.

"A shower. We don't have a bathtub in the shelter restrooms, just showers," I answered.

"Okay, deal."

Derrick was taken to the shelter building and set up with
a room and some clean clothes. He took a shower and
had a meal. The first night in, he didn't watch TV or talk
to many other kids. I checked on him before I left to go
home that night, and he was in bed asleep by 8 p.m.

It was tough living on the streets those days for an
almost 17-year-old boy who thinks he is invincible.

Derrick is 16 ½ years old. He got suspended from school for
carrying a concealed weapon (a pocket knife); no charges
were filed. He has a good academic record in school and had
only one fight this past year. He was in an adolescent psych
treatment program at age 12. His treatment issues included
manic depression, chemical abuse, abandonment issues, anger
issues and problems accepting responsibility. Since an 8-
month in-patient psych treatment program, he has been in and
out of counseling for 4 years. Derrick's psychological issues
began approximately the same time his parents divorced.

Derrick has a history of runaway episodes.

His biological parents are divorced and his mother has
remarried. Derrick has not had any contact with his
biological father for 8 years, but reports getting along
with his stepfather better than he does his mom.

He has one older sister who lives in New York,
and Derrick has a "plan" to move to New York,
live with his sister and become an actor.

He came to the shelter after having been on the streets for
several months. He had no permanent residence and the last
"real bed" he spent the night in was at the Men's Night Shelter
downtown. (And he lied about his age to get in there.) The
biggest drug abuse issue he admits to is smoking cigarettes.

During his intake interview, Derrick expressed his needs and goals.

"I can't take it! Sleeping with those guys downtown. Man, they are dirty and they roll ya at night. I never sleep when I go there. My eyes are slits at night … watching to see if one of 'em is gonna sneak up on me and steal my shoes or cut my throat," he states, staring out one of the many windows in the therapy room

"Do you really think someone might try to kill you there at night?" I asked.

"Sure, if they think you have any money or junk on ya. Sometimes in the night, I have seen them take guys' shoes … you know, boots especially," he said matter-of-factly.

"I need some real food. I get sick all the time lately," he continued. "I just want to get my GED and move to New York with my sister. She said I could come and stay with her."

"Okay, to get you into the program, I have some questions for you and papers about the rules you must follow. Are you ready to start?" I asked.

"Sure, shoot," he snickered. "I mean not really shoot, you know, ask what you want."

"Do you feel like you have been abused or neglected by your mother?"

Quickly, he replied, "Nope."

"Do you feel like you have been abused by your father?"

"Yes, he left me and hasn't even talked to me in eight years. I am his son, you know," he answered defiantly.

"Do you feel like you have been abused or
neglected by your stepfather?"

"No. We get along okay, especially when my
mom isn't around," he answered.

"Tell me about yourself, Derrick. Your friends … your
interests … problems," I asked as I began to write notes.

"Ha, ha, ha … that might take hours, you
know, Ms. U," he kind of laughed.

"Let's see how long it takes to tell your 16 ½ year
history, Derrick. I'm ready to listen."

"I sort of hate my life. Well, my life right now is better than 24
hours ago. Not knowin' where you're gonna sleep or where you're
gonna get some food, I hate. I don't want to live at home any
more 'cause I want more freedom. You know, I want independence
from their rules. But we did eat out quite a lot, and I liked that."

"What about your friends?" I asked as I
looked up at him from my notepad.

"I … I … I don't have many friends. Maybe one or two my
own age. The rest of what you might call my friends are 'street
people' I hang with. I'm not close to many people. I guess the
best friend I have is my sister,when I get to see or talk to her.
I don't trust people. They get on my nerves. You know, most
people are stupid, and I hate stupid people. Someday, I'll show
'em all. You wait and see. I'm gonna' be famous and rich."

There was a long pause. I looked up and Derrick was rolling
his head back on the sofa, rubbing his temples. His hair
was cleaner today, and the sunken dark circles under his
green eyes were less prominent. A peaceful, safe night of
sleep does wonders for a person, I thought to myself.

I redirected him. "You have a steady
girlfriend?" I asked with a smile.

"Nope," he answered quickly.

A long pause before I asked another question,
"What do you do for fun?"

"I go to the library and read. Can you believe that? Sounds weird,
huh? I walk around and walk around. I might hang with some
street folk for awhile and listen to some music if someone has a
radio. We chill…. And no, I haven't used any drugs in almost a
year. Drank some beer sometimes, when I could get some. You
know, beg for money downtown. Then get some jerk to buy me a
bottle for a buck or two. I usually get carded when I try to buy it,
and I ain't go no ID. So I bribe someone or pay 'em to get it for me.

"I never been into gangs, and I don't like crowds.
A loner is what most call me," he said.

"What about school?" I asked.

"I hated it, 'cause it was boring. Because it's so easy.
My hardest subject was biology, but I liked it. History
I really hate. What a waste, pure waste of my time
… school, I mean," his words were hard.

"Tell me about the school rules and your teachers," I probed.

"Hate school, hate most all teachers, hate all principals. I just
wanna go to New York and be an actor, or maybe a model. Make
a lot of money and have fun," he kept staring out one of the open
windows as the breeze blew the white curtains around the casing.

"You need to be able to play by the rules, set up goals and then accomplish them to be and stay in the program here," I said to him. "In fact, Derrick, anywhere you go there are rules."

"I can follow rules, when I want to. I just hate cops though. You know, they have such bad attitudes. I have watched how they treat homeless people. This is America, right?! Even the homeless have rights. The street preacher and the Bible I been readin' seem to be at odds, too! The Bible says to treat everyone as if they were your 'brother' or 'sister.' I don't see the people with authority doing that. So I see some rules are for some people, and there are other rules for other people. Kinda confusing! So whose rules are the truth? Whose rules are right?" he asked me with deep intent in his green eyes that pierced my eyes and into my soul.

"The rules here in this program are: 1. no drugs, 2. get a job, 3. save 25% of your wages in a savings account, 4. get your GED, 5. make all group meetings with your counselor, 6. set a budget and stick to it. Think you can do it?" I looked him straight in the eyes when I asked.

"I'll give it my best. I want off the street. Man, I hate it out there. I hate eatin' 'road kill' and I'm sick of PBJ sandwiches. I want a car, wheels, my own space ... my rules," he said loudly.

Derrick was a survivor and he knew how to manage on the streets. Living on the edge grew old for this middle class boy who had wandered through the city, looking in dumpsters for food. He was tired of sleeping in boxes with newspapers for blankets. Take a spit bath in the public library restroom was dehumanizing for a boy who had always had his own bathroom. Begging for money on street corners and learning from old pros how to panhandle was not the future he wanted.

He was scared, defiant, proud, angry, tired and smart enough to know a dead-end when he faced it day in and day out.

The emergency youth shelter was only a bandage. A 30-day stay to stabilize emotionally, and then for most kids, we plunk them right back into the old situation at home. For Derrick, the Transitional Living Program offered another more viable option. Instead of returning to the home he had run away from repeatedly and then finally been banished from home by Mom, he had a new plan.

The Transitional Living Program offered him 18 months of assisted living in his own apartment, help securing a job, assistance getting his GED, life skills management training (budgeting, banking, housekeeping, etc.) and continued counseling with an adolescent support group. It was 18 months of consistent support financially, emotionally, physically and spiritually — not 2 weeks of stop-gap intervention counseling, not 6 weeks of cognitive therapy, not in-patient treatment at "nice to be here land, but this ain't reality." It was 18 months of support and motivation and attention that made the difference in Derrick's life!! Listen and remember his story.

The 2-mile hike to freedom for Derrick placed him on the road to his dreams and pulled him out of the vicious cycle of hopelessness.

Unfortunately, the funding for these types of programs was stopped by the government. Today, more adolescents than ever wander the streets searching dumpsters and sleeping in pipes at construction sites or boxes in alleys. Or they turn to using or selling drugs just to survive or become prostitutes!

GYPSY'S STORY

"Learning is the result of listening, which in turn leads to even better listening and attentiveness to the other person. In other words, to learn from the child, we must have empathy, and empathy grows as we learn." - Alice Miller

"Lanni, is the coffee ready?" I yelled as I pushed open the door to my sterile white office. The elevator ride up to the tenth floor was not fun at 8 a.m., and we knew one day it would stop — kerplunk! — between floors. It rattled and shook when it started and always stopped 3 to 4 inches above the floor edge. Oh, heck, it made life an adventure at this decaying 15-story building in the heart of downtown.

"Yes, Ms. U, it's ready and there is some real creamer today, not that dry stuff you hate," she answered, sifting through the mail. "You got a lot of mail today."

"I'm sure the end of the month is coming and everyone is catching up on reports. Everybody wants something, a last-minute site visit or an imperative assessment of a kid we have assessed five times," I said as I dropped my briefcase on the desk and headed toward the coffee pot.

"Hey, Lanni, we got a new coffee maker!" I said with real joy in my words. The last one walked across the parking lot with one of the twelfth-floor clients. We were looking out the window of the conference room at the weather Friday after a meeting, and there in the parking lot was "Willie

Winkle" (a weekly M.H. customer of the free clinic), carrying
the coffee maker as quickly as he could off the grounds!

"Yep," she replied. "They must have 20 new ones in
the basement waiting for a new home. Maybe clients
get them as going-away gifts," she chuckled.

I made my cup of java and went back to my desk. The list of
clients was long today. Working Juvenile Services always dictated
a large case load … too large of a case load. I began to open
mail when the commotion began out in the waiting area.

"I gotta see her! I mean now!" a teenage male voice (not
quite deep and not quite tenor) screamed defiantly.

I got up from my desk and went out to
the waiting and check-in area.

"What's going on out here?" I said, staring directly into
the eyes of "Gypsy." There he stood in his grungy decaying
clothes and matted, filthy blonde hair. He still had on
his combat boots, three sizes too large, he had won in
a street "truth or dare" game several months back.

"Damn, Ms. U. I gotta see ya. They're comin' to get me. Please,
I gotta talk to ya, like now," he said loudly as he nervously
looked out the window by the door into the office hallway.

"Who is coming for you, Gypsy?" I asked.

"Them Indians from the graveyard. I saw 'em followin' me.
Had to sleep in the pipes last night, but I had protection,
see," he whipped out a small black handgun.

I saw Lanni's face freeze and fear gripped her big
brown eyes. It startled me, too. It's not everyday some

wild 16-year-old runaway walks into your office and
brazenly pulls a gun and starts waving it around.

"Gypsy, what are you doing with that? You know you cannot bring
a weapon into this building or this office," I said with forceful
intent in my voice, while trying not to be overly threatening to him.

"Ms. U, Ms. U. it ain't loaded. I left the bullets outside in a
bush. I'm not stupid, you know. Jus wanna prove how bad it
is out there by myself at night. Gotta have protection in the
night. It gets so dark, so dark and the bums, they try to get
ya. Tried to pull my boots right off my feet one night. I had
a knife, but that ain't no good protection. Cool, huh? Jus
like on TV!" he kept jabbering. "But them Indians...."

Finally, his voice fell a few bars in sound level and his speech
began to slow down. His anxiety started to dissipate.

"You want some coffee, Gypsy?" I asked, looking at Lanni
and motioning with my eyes for her to get him a cup.

"Oh, cool. I mean hot coffee. Yeah, with lots of sugar, four big
spoonfuls. Love my coffee with sugar," he said. Now the gun
was dangling from his hand and pointing down at the floor.

"Leave the gun on Lanni's desk and come into my office. Lanni
will bring you some coffee and we can talk about what has you so
agitated this morning. You are supposed to make an appointment
to talk with me, you know," I looked him square in the eyes.

"Ms. U, I ain't leavin' my piece with nobody. Look, check it
out. It ain't got no bullets in it, see," he said, holding up the gun
and opening the bullet chamber. "Here, you hold it and see."

He handed me what appeared to be a rather old snub nosed
22 pistol. I checked the barrel and chamber — no bullets.

"We will place this in a drawer while we talk. I do not like guns, and I do not want one staring me in the face when you talk with me," I said matter-of-factly. "Deal?"

"Uhhhhhhhh ... you gonna let me take it back?" he stammered like a little boy caught doing something bad.

"We will see. It is against the law to have a concealed weapon without a license," I said as if he cared. And I know he did not. "Besides, you are under age to have a handgun. Where did you get this? I really do not want to know the answer to that, do I?" I queried.

"Well, probably not, Ms. U. Can we talk now?

I put the gun in a desk drawer. Lanni came in with the cup of coffee and some extra sugar packets in case our young friend wanted it sweeter. The fear was gone from her countenance, and she half-smiled at me as she left the room.

"Okay, what do you want, Gypsy?" I asked sipping on my coffee.

"Hmmm ... uhhh ... I gotta go soon, Ms. U," he took a little sip of the steaming brew and then added another packet of sugar.

"Really? Go where? Do you have any money?" I asked.

"Nope, don't need no money where I'm headed. I can't sleep in those pipes anymore. My feet are hurtin' me and I want something good to eat.... And the Indians are gonna get me," he said, taking another sip of the hot coffee.

"Then let us talk about you going home. I know your mother would welcome you."

"Yeah, for about 10 minutes she would welcome me. Then that damn teletubby husband of hers will start yellin' at me and at

her for me bein' there. I'm tired of him, the b------ ain't my
daddy. He can't tell me s---! I really wanna spit in his face
one more time," he shook his matted hair out of his eyes, as
he spoke. "I ain't never goin' back there to live … never. She
don't want me there. She raised me, she said, and I'm old
enough to take care of myself. They both told me that!"

"Okay, well, why are you here today?"

"Ms. U … I need your help," he said in a little boy voice. "I
think I'm … I … I … I'm not … Ms. U … I think I'm dyin'.'"

He turned his face away from me and the words
trailed off. This was one of those "Oh, my god"
moments, I thought. What do you say next?

Nothing. Let the silence speak for you. Let the heaviness of
the energy in the room set the tone. Listen and be still!

Gypsy just stared intensely at the picture on my wall
of a cop sitting down on the curb with a little girl. It
was a real photo I won at a raffle, and it always drew
people's attention to it. The silence seemed to last a very
long time (in reality, perhaps four or five minutes).

"Nobody cares about me…. You know that, right? I am 'Gypsy,'
the free spirit with no attachments to this world or any other. I am
smart and can out-think most of the guys down in the pipes or over
at the shelter. I got my smokes, no rules, no," his voice became sad
and he turned to face me. It looked like tears were forming in his
blue eyes, which were half covered by his dog mange matted bangs.

"People do care about you, Gypsy. I care," I said quietly,
not wanting to make my words sound unreal.

"I don't think I'm gonna be here a long time … ya know what
I mean? There's a darkness in my mind and it has crawled into

my heart now. I'm gonna die ... I'm gonna die, and it don't really matter. Nope, it don't matter," he said, his eyes falling to the floor and his head bent down to his knees. "Them ... one of them will get me. I know it inside of me, and the owl in my dreams keeps telling me, run, Gypsy, run. Then I wake up, my heart beatin' fast and my hands real sweaty. (A pause again.) My feet really hurt bad, Ms. U. I took my boots off yesterday and some of my toes ... some of 'em are black and I don't feel nothin' when I touch 'em."

He reached down to his boots, as if to pull one off.

"Hold on, kiddo. I'm not a doctor," I said, trying to stop him from contaminating my office with foot odor, which I'm sure would have overwhelmed us both in such a small room.

"I know you ain't a doctor, but I need ya to see my toes. I think they're gonna rot and fall off my feet or somethin'. Please, let me show you. If my toes fall off, I know I won't be able to walk and then I will die, just die," he said, looking at me as he bent over to pull one boot off.

"I said wait! Gypsy ... you can go to the clinic in the next building and show them. Not me! I'll call Florence for you and maybe, if you don't curse at her or the staff, they will check you out."

He sat up in the chair and stared at me. "Ya don't like stinky feet, huh, Ms. U?!"

I looked at him trying to keep from laughing, "Nope, not really. Gypsy, I am not a medical doctor or nurse."

"Okay, okay, but will ya call 'em for me?"

"Yes, no problem. When you are ready to leave here, I will call Florence and see if they can fit you in. You usually need to make an appointment there, too!" I replied.

He kind of tossed a crooked smile my way. What a strange lost young person Gypsy was. No one would believe he was from a middle class family in suburban America, had been an A/B student and gifted artist in school. Once he started smoking pot and huffing spray paint, his life changed. He had been in adolescent chemical dependency treatment programs 11 times ... until his mother's insurance ran out.

I was sure he had lost count how many times he had been in the county jail and detox center. First, he would just stay out all night partying and drugging. Then he would be gone for entire weekends. When confronted by his mother and teachers, he was defiant, very aggressively and verbally abusive to them all. I knew he was on a self-destructive course when he first came to my office. Some friend from school who he had used to get high with (who was now clean and a client of mine) dared him to see me. Gypsy, being the king of "truth or dare," took the dare. That was 6 months ago.

"Is that why you wanted to talk to me? I mean, about your feet?" I asked.

"Nope ... I ... I ... came to tell ya that I'm a walkin' dead guy, and I wanted to thank you for tryin to help me. I know you don't get any money for seen' me all these times. You're okay, just like Misha told me ... cool, Ms. U," he smirked and kind of laughed a small chuckle.

"Well, thank you, I think," I said to him. "Why do you think you're a 'walking dead guy'?"

He slumped back in the chair and rested his head on his left shoulder and folded in really bruised and battered hands on his lap. Then he took a very deep breath, "I seen the Indians. They are in my dreams with the white owl and they are comin' for me. It's my time, Ms. U. It's my time.

135

I got no good reason to stay on this planet no more. And I
don't want them Indians to skin me and take my hair!"

He started getting anxious and his voice got louder
as he spoke. He gripped the arms of the chair.

"Gypsy, have you been using this morning?" I asked,
trying to look at his eyes to check his pupils. It was hard
to see them because of the hair in his face and eyes.

"My usual stop by the gas station, you know. I had my
gas rag in my pocket and I got the leftovers from the
pumps. I left my rag with the bullets in the bushes outside,
didn't want to stink up your place," he answered.

"Oh, you thought you would try and lie to me about using,
right?" I said directly. When caught, he would always
tell me the truth — at least his version of the truth.

"Yep, ya got me, Ms. U. I love that gasoline ... and
gasoline loves me," he said sarcastically back to me.

"You do know, but I will tell you again, probably for the hundredth
time, huffing will kill your brain and ultimately YOU!"

"I know ... I know ... but like I said, I'm a walking dead guy. It's
only a matter of time. I just came here to see ya, Ms. U. I been in
all kinds of treatment programs and I been to lots of counselors.
I been to jail ... detention ... boot camp, you name it. You know
all that. I'm sure my file is pretty thick," he chuckled to himself.
"At least you will remember me, right, Ms. U? You will remember
my face, right? You will know I was...," his voice got quiet and
he began to whisper, "I never fit. I never belonged anywhere.
All I remember about my life is my dad leavin' one night after
beatin' Mom till she cried. He left and we never seen him again.
I remember my mom screamin' at me all the time. Never did I do
anything right. It was scary at night in the house 'cause she was

gone on dates or partying all the time. I would draw things ...
pages and pages of pictures. One teacher said I had a gift. Boy, he
was a loser. The only thing I'm good at is bein' a pain in the a--.
I'm tired, Ms. U. I don't have friends anymore. I sleep any place
that's dry for the night. When I get rained on, well, that's the
only time my clothes get a washin' and I get a shower. I smoke
cigarette butts off the street or out of ash trays. You know, I've
worn these same clothes for over 2 months. I stink really bad, don't
I?" he stopped talking for a moment and just stared into my face.

"They're comin' for me, those Indians I saw at the graveyard a
couple of weeks ago. Yeah, I slept in a graveyard. Cool, huh?
I saw 'em come up from the ground and then they saw me.
They yelled and started after me. I ran and ran till I couldn't
make my legs move. I collapsed, and guess where I was? When
I woke up, I was outside this building in the bushes. Guess I
knew it was safe here. Those Indians wouldn't come here."

He stopped talking and drank the rest of the coffee. I watched him
sit there hunched over the Styrofoam cup and wondered. Why
him? What happened in his mind and his spirit that made him
give up, or was it give in? Many kids have something in them that
creates a way to compartmentalize trauma ... stress ... abuse ...
neglect. Not this boy. He was one of the fragile kids, or as I call
them, "Glass Soul Kids." These are children whose precious inner
self is cracked and chipped early in life. When they grow, their soul
is like a fragile piece of glass. Remember a piece of glass, maybe
a vase or dish your grandmother held precious and you couldn't
understand why? It was cracked and chipped, useless piece of glass,
right? Then one day, you slammed it too hard on the table and it
shattered into a zillion tiny fragments. Your grandmother gasped
but tried not to show her anguish over the cherished piece of glass.
She told you it would be all right, not to worry, it was just a piece
of glass. You tried to gather the zillion pieces of glass together to
fix the old thing. But you couldn't even find all the pieces, there
were so many small splinters and fragments. But Grandmother

hugged you and smiled. You felt better; after all, it was just a
worthless piece of glass. You would buy her a new vase someday.

"I gotta go, Ms. U," Gypsy said suddenly. He tossed the
empty coffee cup into my trash can. "Five points for me."

"I still don't get why you had to talk with me
today, Gypsy," I said, wondering.

"Uhhh, needed to see ya. Tell ya about the Indians and thank you.
You know. You know ... for never chargin' me. You're probably
a pretty expensive counselor. Don't have much time, Ms. U,
and I've wasted a lot of my life already, and it's a short one," he
sounded older now, almost like a seer predicting his future.

"I see. Want me to call the clinic now?" I asked.

"Sure, Ms. U."

I picked up the phone and called the free county clinic in
the building next door. I asked for Florence. When she came
on the line, I quickly told her the situation, and as usual,
she said she could fit him in. I thanked her and hung up.

"Gypsy ... Gypsy ... Gypsy, what should we do with you? You
are a smart, gifted compassionate and gentle one of God's soft
souls. You are wandering through dark streets and wallowing
in the mire of what was not nor can be. How can I help you get
a grip?" I asked in bewilderment, because I liked this kid, and
you cannot say that about every teen that crosses your path.

"Ms. U, just don't forget me. You already helped me.
You kept the Indians from getting me today," he
answered as he stood up. "I need my gun back, Ms. U.
Please let me have a fightin' chance," he pleaded.

"Gypsy, I would be breaking the law to let you have that
gun back. You cannot have it in the clinic anyway."

"Ms. U, I won't last another night without it.
It's my protection. It's my safety."

"You go to the clinic first, and then come back. We will deal with
the gun issue at that time," I said hoping he would go for it.

He thought about it and then looked me straight in the
eyes and said, "You always been straight with me. You been
cool, so I'll go to the clinic without my gun. 'Cause they
for sure would take it from me. But I'll be back for it when
I'm done," he said, holding out his hand to shake mine.

I took his rough, dirty hand between both of mine, "You
need to stop the gas. It will kill you before the Indians do."

I rubbed his hand for a moment and watched his dilated
eyes well up with tears, but they never spilled out.

"Now, go next door and let Florence see your
feet," I said as I let go of his hand.

He turned toward the door, pushed his mangy hair from
his eyes and then stopped and looked back at me.

"You'll be here when I'm done," he asked.

"Right here," I said, planting my feet and smiling.

He left the office while Lanni got out the Lysol and air freshener.

Florence called me later in the morning. Gypsy had been taken
to the hospital. Six toes were to be removed because he had
gangrene. He called me from the hospital once and told me
his mom was there. That was a good thing. I would never hear
from Gypsy again after that conversation. The gun remained
in the desk drawer, and I do not know if the Indians won.

JORDAN'S STORY

"Children begin by loving their parents; as they grow older, they judge them; sometimes they forgive them." - Oscar Wilde

Jordan was a beautiful azure-eyed 10-year-old girl with long copper red curly hair that framed her cherubic face. My first impression of this quiet child was that she should have been a model for children's clothes or some great toy store. She was very solemn at our meeting and never connected her eyes to mine. Those beautiful wide eyes seemed somehow remote and distant, always staring off into space, never near.

Jordan's story is difficult to tell, and it was extremely difficult for her to process or know how to tell it.

One day, she told a friend at school about her father touching her and making her cry. The school friend told the teacher about Jordan's story. The teacher spoke to Jordan, who broke down and cried — not just because of what happened to her, but because she was afraid of what might happen now that the secret was uncovered!

The teacher called Children's Protective Services hotline.

The CPS worker went to the school to interview Jordan and didn't know what to believe. Jordan recanted her story about her father, saying it was a dream she made up. But the teacher and Jordan's friend both said it wasn't a dream. They believed Jordan had told them the truth and was now scared. They believed Jordan had been raped by her father, and Jordan was scared because the "secret" was out.

I began my session with Jordan at the CPS office. Later, many months later, I would move them to the local Dairy Queen (my favorite office location — well, maybe my second favorite). Kids eating ice cream seems to make for great conversation. I have not quite figured out why ice cream did the trick, but it always worked. After a marshmallow sundae or a banana split, they would talk, relax and breathe, exhaling breaths that would divulge deep secrets held in tight.

It took eight months to finally break into the depths of this child and the family secrets each member held within.

Her mother was in denial that her estranged husband (who had already served one prison term for raping Jordan when she was 4 years old), whom she let back into her life, was doing anything to Jordan. She believed he did his time for his past crime and now was different, a new man. Jordan was lying and making up stories about him, she said.

This mother was not supportive of her daughter in any way. She stood by her man! Plus she had a new baby to contend with. While Jordan's dad had been in prison for 4 years for the conviction of raping his 4-year-old daughter, Mom had found a new boyfriend.

She got pregnant and had another little girl, Callie. But Callie's father beat her, and she had kicked him out when her estranged husband got out of prison. (Sounds like a "Jerry Springer Show." Life is stranger than TV!)

"Well, Jordan, shall we go for ice cream today?" I asked as the pretty little girl came into my office.

"I would like that. It's very hot outside today," she replied, very matter of fact.

We left the office, walked to my car and sped off to
the Dairy Queen. Once there, we found our favorite
booth. Jordan sat down, and I went to the counter.

Halfway through our chilly snack, she began to
talk. "I really love ice cream, you know."

"I seem to understand that," I said with a smile. "You really
like coming here better than the park, don't you?"

"Yeah! The only time I get ice cream is with you. My
mother says we can't afford it. Money is scarce because
of the baby, and Daddy doesn't have a job, yet."

"Hmmm. Well, then, it's a good thing I came along
to take you to the Dairy Queen," I said.

There was a long silence as we both ate our
sundaes. Finally, it was broken by Jordan.

"I need to ask you something, Miss Pam," she said,
without looking up from her ice cream.

"Sure, Jordan. Ask me."

"Is it true that fathers can do anything to their kids? ... I
mean, is it a rule? They can do to us what they want?"

"You know that isn't true, Jordan. Your father just came out of
jail because he did things to you he should not have done," I said,
looking at her. But she would not raise up her face, no eye contact.

"I don't remember before ... I was too little ... and he and
Mommy told me it was all a mistake." She kept eating her
ice cream, her face down while talking to the table.

"Jordan, you were very little, but there is a lot of evidence, proof, that your dad did things to you he should not have done," I explained.

"Well, I know what he does to me now. He comes in my bedroom at night, and he makes me do things."

This was going to be the "talkie day" (some call it a breakthrough moment) with Jordan. She trusted me enough to open her heart and spirit to me. This was not going to be just a head talk day or chatter session.

"Did you tell your mom when these things happened?" I queried.

"I tried. She told me I was crazy, or I was dreaming, or she just told me to shut up!"

"So you told your friend at school? I know it's hard to think about stuff like that and you need someone to talk to," I said.

"Yeah. He kept coming in my room every night, making me touch him and kiss him. He loves me, I know. And I missed him when he was gone. Mom's boyfriend Rob never touched me. He was drunk all the time, and he was mean to Mommy. He never made me touch him though. Once Daddy came back, it has been better," she said.

"Better how?"

"No more screaming or hollering. The baby cries at night, but Mommy and Daddy don't fight. Mommy is tired a lot, and Daddy wants to let her sleep. That's why he comes to sleep with me ... you know, so Mommy can sleep."

"Couldn't he sleep in another room or on the sofa?" I asked.

"I guess so, but he says I am his and he can do what he wants with me. I belong to him," she said.

"I see…. So why did you tell your friend at school you were afraid of him and he had done bad things to you?"

"'Cause, 'cause, it does hurt sometimes. Not every time … just when he puts his fingers in me it hurts a lot, and his fingers are big. But he tells me it is only for a minute, and the hurt will go away. He says he is making me ready for boyfriends. And it makes him feel good. I make him feel good."

"Jordan, adults, not even Daddies, should touch children in certain ways. How does it make you feel when he touches you?"

"Scared, kinda. He tells me not to tell Mommy or anybody. It is our secret, and I belong to him, so he can do what he wants to me. I really don't like it. I really don't like … when he makes me kiss on him," she said.

Jordan was talking at a pretty fast pace today. Why was today confession day? I don't know. Maybe enough moments of time had occurred between us for her to trust me, Or maybe another incident with her father had happened. Whichever, I had the conversation that would now either pull her out of the home or push her father out.

The choice would be her mother's. Sexual abuse was happening in this family, and finally, somebody was listening. So should her mother. Failure to protect would be grounds to remove Jordan.

"Miss Pam, why do you come talk with me every week?" Jordan looked up at me with those pleading blue eyes.

"Why do you think I am here, Jordan?" I asked.

"'Cause my social worker thinks I need a counselor, and I'm messed up because my father abuses me," she said, looking directly at me.

Whoa! Where is God when you need some moral support?
Kids have the most direct way of getting to the heart of things sometimes. Are they innocently direct or directly innocent?
Good question. I am not sure myself, but I know I have had to face years of such blunt, "in-your-face" questions from kids.

"Jordan, you are very smart. Do you believe your father is abusing you? Is he making you do things you would not do with other people ... other men?" May as well be direct with the child, especially if this is a test, I thought.

A sudden change in her countenance occurred. "Yes, I don't want to do the things he wants me to do. I feel funny when we are in my bed and he makes me touch him. Sticky stuff gets all over my sheets and I feel dirty.....," she said. Her eyes were filling with water as she brushed the copper tendrils from her face. "He doesn't touch the baby the way he touches me."

"How do you know?" I asked.

"'Cause he told me. Callie isn't his, and so he can't touch her like he touches me. I belong to him, so he can do things to me, he says." Now tears were gently falling down her cheeks. "They play with Callie and cuddle her. Mom just yells all the time at me. He tells her to shut up and leave me alone, but she keeps on."

"Have you told you mother about your dad touching you and making you do things you don't want to?" I asked.

"Yes. She says I am lying. Daddy went to prison once and I should shut up and not lie about him 'cause I'm mad at Callie."

"Are you mad about Callie?" I asked.

"No! I love her. I hold her and play with her a lot," she said with a tone of joy in her voice. "She is better than a doll to play with."

"You aren't unhappy because your mother had another baby?" I asked cautiously.

"I change her diapers … feed her … wash her … lots of things, 'cause Mommy doesn't feel good a lot of the time. She sleeps a lot, so I watch her and do stuff with her. I do love her. She is better than a doll, really and truly." She seemed to lighten up with she spoke of her sister. "Mommy is sick a lot and I have to help with Callie, but I do it because I want to, not because Mommy wants me to."

The air was silent for a long moment as we finished our ice cream. Then I broke the quiet with another question: "So you believe your dad doesn't touch Callie in the same way he touches you?"

"No, she isn't his, and he is afraid of her real daddy! He might come and kill my daddy if he touched her like he does me. No, he just loves on her normal, that's all."

"Do you want to stay at your house with your mom and Callie," I asked.

"Yeah. I don't want to go anywhere else. I just want Daddy to stop touching me and making me touch him. Can you … can you make him stop?" she asked.

Her tears stopped now, and she was squirming in the hard seat. A chocolate ice cream ring circled her lips, so I told her to go to the restroom and wipe her face. When she returned from the restroom, her smile was back and the moment to talk about deep feelings had passed.

I had to take her back to her home — to a mother who didn't listen and a father who felt she was his property to do with as he saw fit. Her words to her school friend and her teacher were not fantasy, not a dream. This child lived in a home where life was distorted and "People of the Lie" (Scott Peck, 1983) rule.

Jordan's story did not end that day. Months of therapy and manipulation by parents and social service workers would trap this little girl in a world of torn loyalties. Lies, traps, cons and malicious games would turn her life upside down. Jordan would survive, but how well was always the question.

And her words have haunted me: "I love my daddy and I don't want him to go to jail again. Please, make him stop doing those things to me, Miss Pam.... Please, make my mommy believe me. Why won't she listen to me? Somebody needs to listen to me!"

It was very interesting that not one time did Jordan say she hated her father, all the months I worked with her. She was afraid of him and afraid she would be the one to cause his return to prison. In her soul, she hated the things she did sexually with him, but her heart loved him. He had convinced her she was his property and he had "rights" with her. When you own something, you can do with it what you choose.

Jo Anna's Story

"Grownups never understand anything for themselves and it is tiresome for children to be always and forever explaining things to them." - Antoine de Saint-Exupery

Jo Anna was a pretty blonde 12-year-old female attending the seventh grade. She was very overweight and constantly intimidated by her younger siblings (a brother and sister) because of her size. She told her teachers in school about verbal abuse she experienced at home from her mom and brother, but they didn't know how to help.

Finally, she opened up to her math teacher about past sexual abuse. The teacher called Family Services, and a case was opened and investigation begun.

She is the eldest of three children and expresses resentment over being the "caretaker" for the family all the time. Dad is missing and hasn't been seen in years. The children call it "missing in action," as he walked out the door one day, never to return. The mother suffers from chronic depression and an inordinate fear of her in-laws appearing and stealing the children from her. The mental health clinic has put her on several anti-depressants. She barely gets by on the welfare check that comes every month and has no extended family support.

During my initial intake interview, Jo Anna quietly began to tell about the "family secret" that consumed them all each day and why they had moved 1,400 miles away from their previous home. She reported that all of the children had been involved in "ritual abuse" with their grandparents being the leaders of a cult. Jo Anna was very expressive relating memories of cult rituals the children were used in. She also stated that she was sexually abused by several of her mother's boyfriends for the past 4 years.

The memories and fears were now spilling into her dreams ... actually, nightmares, each time she closed her eyes. Jo Anna has a great deal of repressed anger that reared out around her mother. She especially "hates being the mother" to everyone. Her reported chores include: doing all the laundry for everyone, cleaning the bathrooms, cooking, taking care of the dogs, making her siblings do their homework, taking care of her mother who is sick in bed almost every day. Jo Anna is defiant and hateful toward her mother, screaming obscenities at her all the time. All the children use four-letter words in their regular conversation with everyone, except teachers at school.

The school reports that she is a good student when she wants to be. Her grades are all passing, but her attendance is irregular. Jo Anna has exceptionally good verbal skills but is extremely immature for her age, emotionally. Her friends at school are two to three years younger than she is. She loves music and art but rarely gets to participate in extra activities because she is always taking care of her family.

Family Services was called in to assess the family, because Jo Anna not only began talking about the abuse in detail but also was threatening suicide to her friends. Several drawings her teachers found startled them and seemed significant expressions of Jo Anna's inner turmoil:

Picture 1 shows a drawing of her present house. It is like a "blueprint" of a home drawn in pencil, no color and black bolts of lightning are drawn striking the outline at all four corners of every room.

Picture 2 is another pencil drawing of her family where her siblings are stick people with no hands, feet or clothes, and she and her mother have shape, feet, hands and clothes on.

These were drawn by a young girl very gifted in art, so her teachers state! They appear to be pictures drawn by a much younger child and one with no appreciable artistic talent, which is not true of Jo Anna.

Family Services workers began to become very scared to visit the family when Jo Anna and her siblings began telling them stories about "witchcraft" and seeing the devil circling their house.

My first visit with Jo Anna was an edgy adventure and that was only the beginning of an incredulous journey with this family. We met at their home on an overcast windy April afternoon I shall never forget! I was accompanied by a Family Services worker, who never returned to the home after the visit.

We walked up a narrow sidewalk after we parked the car on a small hill. As we approached the house, three heads appeared in the windows and three sets of eyes followed us as we walked up the street to the house. They followed us up the pathway to the front door, and Jennifer knocked. It was a small two-story frame house that needed to be painted. The broken windows were stuffed with cloth. The door opened as I reached to knock when no one responded to Jennifer's weak tap.

"Hello," a very tall, extremely thin, long and dark-haired woman dressed in black pants and a black sweater said, as she opened the door for us to come in. "I am Rue _____. I ... we been expectin' y'all."

"Thank you," I replied as we entered the dark, shadowy room. Curtains were closed and only one dim lamp was on. It was still afternoon outside, but inside you couldn't tell. The wallpaper was a dark maroon, and the hardwood

151

floor looked like it had been painted a dark reddish brown,
so the room was ominously full of dark shadows.

One picture was on the wall near a window. A picture of
Jesus with a heart painted on his chest and a halo of thorns
around his head stood out from the dingy surroundings
and seemed out of place. Literally, 50 crosses were scattered
on the walls and doorways in the room we could see.

"Here, have a seat on the sofa," she said, motioning to a dark
brown fuzzy piece of furniture that looked like it came from
the 1930s. Not inviting to sit on, I thought, but we did.

"Mrs. _____, I came today to introduce Ms. Uher; she is going to
be your new family counselor and work with Jo Anna … and all of
your family, actually," said Jennifer, the Family Services worker.

"Good, we need some help, don't we," she said, smiling vacantly.

"Well, the school and the court are concerned about your children,
Mrs. _____. Jude is in trouble with the police every other week
for something (he was the 11-year-old boy). Kit is skipping classes
constantly and scaring other kids at school with stories … you
know, stories about the devil and all. (Kit was the 8-year-old
younger sister). And Jo Anna … gosh, Mrs. _____, Jo Anna is
now saying to her teachers she wants to kill herself!" The Family
Service worker was worn out just from explaining the situation.

"Oh, she don't mean it. She's jus talkin'. You know how
kids are. One day they hate ya, the next day they love
ya," Mrs. _____ replied calmly with a very flat affect
in her voice and that vacant gaze in her eyes.

"Well, Mrs. _____, the court and Family Services take this
whole situation very seriously. We have records of phone calls
from you asking for help and reporting that your two youngest
children are out of control. Jude has been before the judge three

times in the past 2 months. Kit is on the streets way past curfew,
and the police report bringing her home 16 times this past
month alone. And now your oldest wants to kill herself? Please,
Mrs. _____, let's get real," Jennifer was exasperated with the
mother's apparent denial of the urgency of the family situation.

I interjected, "Mrs. _____, you could lose your children
if we do not try to make this home a safer place where
… you, the parent, are in control and respected."

She stared or maybe glared at me. She was severe looking, probably
in her late thirties, but the lines on her face made her appear much
older. Her body repositioned, and she seemed more attentive.

"I see. You want to take my kids away. Well, they love
me, no matter everything. They don't want ta' leave
me. Ask 'em and see," she was getting upset. Good,
I thought, at least she was capable of emotion.

"No, Mrs. _____, the whole point of this therapy
is to keep the kids with you. You are their mother
… their family," I said very matter of fact.

"It's hard bein' a single parent and the kids been through a lot.
Movin' so much and their daddy, he took off an' left us," she
put her head in her hands as she spoke. "I'm tired all the time
… guess it's the medicine. I got anti-depressants and I don't
feel like eatin' much and I don't sleep well these days. But I
know that ain't an excuse when it comes to my kids. I want your
help. We want your help. We need lots of prayer and more."

"Great, I will start with Jo Anna next week and
see the other children every other week, and once a
month we will have a family session here in the living
room. That seems to be a good way to start."

And with that said, it was time to see the kids briefly and leave. This place was oppressively depressing and the air smelled bad. It was more than a musty dirt smell. I wasn't sure, but it almost smelled like incense or maybe pot.

"Let me get the kids. They are upstairs waiting," she said as she rose from the chair and headed toward the stairway.

"Whew! Let's get this over fast," Jennifer said. "This place gives me the creeps. I mean it feels bad, smells bad, looks bad and has an energy I don't like."

I looked at her rubbing her arms, as if she had caught something sitting here. "I know it gives off the energy of residents and that is very dark. Not a good thing," I replied back to her.

Moments later, the kids came tearing down the stairs like a herd of wild animals let loose. I introduced myself to them as they all tried to talk at the same time. Their mother stood, watching them. She seemed tired; maybe it was her medication, making her appear listless and ready for bed.

The children were full of anxious energy. They were in wrinkled clothes that looked like they had been slept in for days. Jude needed a haircut and a pair of sneakers that didn't have holes. Kit had auburn hair down to her shoulders and chubby cheeks with a big smile. Jo Anna was a tall overweight preteen with sad green eyes and teeth that needed braces. This would be a challenge — how much of one I did not realize until several months into therapy with them.

My first individual session with Jo Anna was enlightening and overwhelming. I picked her up at school, and we went to one of my special therapy places: the park. She seemed to like the idea.

"So, tell me about yourself," I said, opening the door to whatever the girl felt she needed to talk about.

"I am scared," she said softly, not looking at me but
gazing at the creek we were sitting next to.

"Scared?" I mirrored back.

"Yeah, I'm scared of the dark. I'm scared of the
devil. I'm scared they will find us and take us
back to where we came from," she replied.

"That's a lot to be frightened of," I said.

"I don't want to go back there ... never. My grandparents are
bad people. Well, they made us do things that were bad. My
mother did them, too! She says she had to 'cause she was afraid."

"Fear can make people do things they never
planned or expected to do, Jo Anna," I said.

"I know, I love my mom, sometimes, but most
times, I'm mad at her," she continued.

"Why?" I asked. It was really strange that she opened up our
first conversation so quickly with intimate feelings, I thought.

"Why?" she stood up and walked toward the creek. "Because
... she ... she makes me do everything. I have to do the
cleaning, the cooking, the laundry, watch the kids and still do
my homework — plus take care of her. She stays in bed all day
and then is up all night. She reads her stupid Bible all night,
as if that will keep them away. I don't know ... maybe it will
keep the devil out of the house. I hate my life, Miss Pam. I
hate it, except for school. I love school and all the teachers."

"That's a good thing, Jo Anna. School is
a safe place for you, isn't it?"

"Yes. I don't have to take care of anybody, but me.
I mean, no chores I hate, just schoolwork."

"What is your favorite subject in school?" I asked genuinely.

"Oh, I like math, but I love art and music. The art teacher and I are
doing some special projects. Math is easy and fun. I'm not so good
at science, but I think it is interesting. I just like going there. This
is the first school we have been in where we will have finished the
whole year and not have moved," she looked at me as she said that.

"You have moved a lot. Why?" I queried.

"'Cause my dad was always getting a new job or
sometimes my mother wanted to get away from my
grandparents and other family," she replied.

"Hmmm. Kind of hard to have friends when you move so much."

"Here I finally have friends. It's great, only I can't bring
them over to my house and I can't go to theirs."

"What about going to a movie or something
at school with your friends?"

"I usually have to take care of my brother and sister
… and mom. Bummer, huh? My mom is sick all
the time. I know she has an illness," she said.

"Yes, depression is a real illness, Jo Anna."

"Not just that! She gets into 'bad stuff' and it makes her
sick with her spirit. That's why we moved here, to get away
from the 'bad people and the bad stuff'," she said.

"What kind of 'bad stuff'?" I asked, wondering
if I really wanted to know.

Jo Anna sat down on the edge of the creek and looked at me intently. "I think I can trust you, Miss Pam. I want to trust somebody. I need to trust somebody." There was a long pause. Jo Anna sighed and took a deep breath that shook her whole body before she started to speak again.

"Grandma wanted to kill Mom. We have seen a lot of bad stuff, Miss Pam. And we done a lot of bad things ... like I steal stuff from the stores all the time. I know, but we don't got any money. I need make-up, and I steal it. That's, okay not really bad stuff. Everybody steals," she said.

"I don't know about that, Jo Anna. Many people do not steal, many kids do not steal. I don't steal."

"You got money!" she was almost shouting at me. Then she calmed down as she watched my reaction.

"If I don't have money for something, I wait until I do," I replied.

"We steal, and we are good at it. Our father taught how not to get caught, and they haven't got me yet. Now, Jude, he's been caught sometimes, but because he is young, they let him go."

"That won't be the case forever, you know. And there is always a first time for everything, like being caught for stealing," I said, trying to make a point.

She shrugged her shoulders. "Maybe, but I am good."

Well, Jo Anna had a confident hard edge beneath the pathetic little girl image she projected. I also began to see how she verbally could be very manipulative with adults.

"Tell me why you and your mom fight so much," I said, trying to get us refocused.

"She yells at us constantly, and she never takes up for me.
She lets Jude call me names, like 'fat hog' or the 'B' word
all the time. Why can't she take my side once in awhile?
After all I slept……..oops," she stopped talking.

"Yes, you slept….?" Would she tell me or wouldn't she. I had
been suspecting she had been sexually abused. Jo Anna was
very provocative for a 12 year old, and her make-up and clothes
seemed more appropriate for a 16-year-old high school girl.

"Listen, I hate her 'cause she made me sleep with her boyfriends.
There, I told you! I had sex with my mother's boyfriends and
my mother knew it. She wanted me to do it. Sick, huh? Who
do you think I can tell that to? God or maybe the devil?"
She was angry and her tone of voice was becoming more
hateful with each mouthful of words she spewed. Tears were
welling up in her eyes, and she turned away from me.

"That's a lot of stuff to keep inside. Have you ever
talked to anybody about this before?," I asked.

"No, never, but I can't just keep it all inside anymore. I hate
her … I hate her … I … hate," she was crying openly now
and not fighting to keep the tears contained inside.

"Cry, Jo Anna. Tears are a way the soul cleans out stuff
we keep bottled up and are afraid to talk about or share
with others," I said, trying to comfort her. Can you
comfort a child who is really not a child any more?

She cried for a long time. Then she walked toward the water and
reached down and put her hands in the creek. She seemed to be
washing away the pain as she cupped the water in her hands and
poured it over her head and face. I was silent and respected her
moment of releasing the suffering and giving it back to the world.

"We need to get you home; it will be dark soon,
and you have school tomorrow and probably
homework," I said, breaking the silence.

"Yes, I always have homework," she replied. "At
least I won't have to cook dinner tonight. She
will have to do that 'cause I'm not there."

"That's what mothers are for sometimes," I said, trying
to move the heavy moment to a lighter-feeling tone.

"Mothers are supposed to protect you, aren't they?"
she shot at me as she spun around and started to
walk back to the bench I was sitting on.

"Yes, they are, Jo Anna. Mothers, fathers, grandparents,
teachers, counselors ... we are all supposed to
help keep you safe and out of harm's way."

She stopped directly in front of me. More anger was pent up
inside this 200-pound, 12-year-old "woman-child," and I could
see it in her face. "Then why did my mom let our grandparents
sell us to the devil?" she said, glaring her now bloodshot eyes
into mine. "Why did we have to do those satanic blood things
with people? Why did she let them touch us? They were
strangers and we were little kids! She let them make us do
really bad things, Miss Pam. Now the devil wants our souls.
Yeah, ask my brother. He sees the devil outside our house at
night. That's why our mother has all those crosses up over the
doorways and pictures of Jesus everywhere in the house. It's to
keep the devil out ... scary. That's why we don't sleep at night,
Miss Pam. That's why we are all afraid of the darkness. That's
why we are bad kids! We are bad kids! We are just bad."

I stood up and took Jo Anna's hands in mine. "These are not bad
hands." I touched her cheeks, wet with tears again. "This is not a
bad face." I wiped with tears with my sleeve and took her chin in

my hand and turned her head toward the sky. "Look, God made your eyes to see, and when it rains, it is not a bad thing. When the sky grows dark at night, God set that in motion and that is not a bad thing. God made you and that is a good thing. Sometimes bad things happen to all of us, and sometimes adults let bad things happen. War is a bad thing. Hating someone because they aren't the same color as you is a bad thing. But once we learn what bad means, we also know what good is — then we can learn to forgive and go on. I do not know why bad things have happened to you and your family. I don't know why your mother and father did not protect you from the bad. I do know you now have people who will help you and protect you, and that is a good thing."

Jo Anna looked at me as she stopped crying.

"I need to leave that place, Miss Pam. I have been thinking about it a long time. I want to go to a foster family. My family is dangerous and it isn't a safe place to live. My brother and sister need help, too! Mom isn't able. She just can't take care of us," Jo Anna said, torn with so many emotions. It would take months to sort them out.

Over the course of the next 6 months, the children all related in depth the "ritual abuse" and sexual abuse that happened to them over the years. Jude would eventually be sent to a psychiatric treatment program because of his skirmishes with the law. Kit was put into foster home because Mom couldn't keep her off the streets at night. Jo Anna went to a temporary foster family until specialists in "ritual abuse" were brought in to help sort through the years and layers of abuse these children had seen and experienced.

It was a horrific journey for them and for those of us working with them. Please believe "ritual abuse" is real and it exists right here in the good old U.S.A. Their mother admitted she could not care for or protect her children and gave them up willingly. Her last message to me was the following:

"Most of the time I am sad because the way my children are. It is hard for me to relax most of the time because I don't know what will happen next. Most of the time I feel tired and I wonder sometimes how I made it this far. It takes me 2-3 hours to go to sleep. I think about everything and wonder why? I am sad because my children talked about the witchcraft and they told about the bodies and animals they saw dead. I feel like at times it didn't happen, but it really did. We didn't go to church then and I didn't make them. I did make them once we got away ... maybe it was too late. I hope this don't happen again. I feel that I turned my back on God and that is hard to forgive that. It is hard to forget about what happened. It is hard to write about it and talk about it. Why did this happen? Why did I let it happen?"

WESLEY'S STORY

"Children don't read to find their identity. They don't read to free
themselves of guilt, to quench their thirst for rebellion, or to get
rid of alienation. They have no use for psychology. The detest
sociology. They still believe in good, the family, angels, devils, witches,
goblins, logic, clarity, punctuation and other such obsolete stuff."
- Isaac Bashevis Singer (1978 Nobel Prize banquet address)

Wesley was a quiet handsome 6 year old with beautiful,
thick coal black hair that curled around his face. He never
smiled and always looked like he was in deep contemplation
or visiting another dimension with his thoughts. He stood
3 feet 4 inches tall and walked with a slight skip to his step
because he had broken his leg as a very young boy and it had
not healed correctly. You would really never know one leg was
2 inches shorter than the other for he compensated with his
clever hop-skip-step gait. What you did notice was that his
fingers twitched, and his hands shook at the wrists when he was
excited. That did not happen very often when we first met.

Wesley was the child that would change my life forever. Because
of his story, I wrote this book. I promised him — and many
other children — that I would someday make people listen.
You see, his mother wouldn't listen ... his father wouldn't listen
... his teachers didn't know how to listen ... and many adults
never took the time to listen. They just thought he was cute!

Today is your time, Wes. Here is your
story. I hope they are listening!

Wesley was referred to me for counseling along with his mother and her new husband (who was not Wesley's dad). When the case came to me, Wesley had been taken from his family and placed in foster care. The plan for Wesley was to reunify him with his mother and step-dad. The problem was the CPS supervisor was a wise woman, and she knew doing that would put Wesley back in harm's way. So she called me and asked for me to assess the case and work with him and his family. It would be 4 months before the final disposition hearing. She wanted another opinion concerning what was in Wesley's best interest.

Wesley had been removed from his family because his teacher at school noticed profound changes in him. One Monday, he came to school, after a long weekend with open sores on his hands and arms. The sores were red and looked infected. When he was sent to the school nurse, they found over 30 open sores on his stomach, legs, arms, shoulders and hands.

The school nurse felt they looked like burns, and when they asked what happened, he wouldn't talk. Nothing came out of his mouth. He just stared into the walls of the room.

His mother was called and asked to come to the school. She came and was shouting mad, stating Wesley was allergic to bugs and he would scratch bug bites until they were raw. The sores were bug bites and nothing more.

Fortunately for Wesley, no one at school believed her. All the bites were the same size and some were raw holes, deep into the skin, almost to the shin bone on his legs.

The nurse stood her ground and called CPS. They came, and off to the hospital Wesley went with a CPS worker and his mother screaming all the way! The doctor at the emergency room agreed with the school nurse. Wesley's sores were not bug bites but burns, and some were seriously infected.

The official report states that the doctor believed they were cigarette burns. Wesley was removed from his family and placed in foster care, while an immediate investigation began.

After a few weeks, Wesley finally told his social worker that his step-dad burned him, but that's all he said. His mother and step-dad denied that was what happened and vowed a fight in court. So time to call in an interventionist counselor, and I entered the picture. Heal the boy who wouldn't talk anymore and find out what happened. Sure!

I met with Wes two times a week for the first 2 months. He was an iceberg. Never cracked a smile or laughed out loud. The only conversation we had was if I asked questions and he politely answered them. Usually, he would answer with a sentence, and on rare subjects, maybe he uttered two sentences.

For the first month, we met at the office in the play therapy room where he would play for an hour with whatever toy he liked that day. Sometimes, I would read to him; he liked that time. His favorite storybook was Pinocchio, and he would ask me to read it to him many times over the weeks and months we met.

When I realized nothing was happening in the office, I started taking him places. We went to Wal-Mart's toy department, and he sort of liked that. He smiled just a little when we got to the action figures.

Next, I tried an Indian Pow Wow, where he wore Indian war paint and learned to dance. This time, he asked questions and wanted to talk to the chief. Progress, I thought; slowly, he was warming up to me.

Someone had really hurt this little boy. His affect to the world was very detached, and he never showed any emotion. No real laughter ... no tears ... no anger ... no expression of loss for being away from his mother, sister and step-dad.

We would go to the park and swing or play in the creek. I took him to my second office, the ice cream store. He loved vanilla ice cream, but still no real conversation. He gave answers to what happened to him or how he felt being in foster care.

He did get supervised visits with his mother and sister several times a week. He seemed happy to see his sister, and sometimes he smiled at his mom. He never looked at his step-dad or spoke to him (red flag). His mother kept saying the sores were bug bites, but he said nothing. The step-dad was as silent as Wesley was at each meeting. We would soon begin family therapy sessions, and he would have to talk.

Then the first breakthrough came. I got a call early one evening from the CPS supervisor about Wesley. She said the foster parents were having problems with Wesley and wanted someone to talk to him. He was being defiant and wouldn't follow their rules, and he had gotten into some trouble with another foster child in the same home. She asked me to go over there and talk with him and find out what was going on.

I drove out to the foster home around 7 p.m, and there was Wesley sitting outside on the porch step. His head was in his hands, and his elbows were bent, resting on his knees.

"Hey, kiddo ... what's going on?" I asked as I walked up to him. He raised his head up slightly but didn't say anything.

"Okay, Wesley, what kind of trouble are you in?" He still didn't speak. I knocked on the door, and the foster mother answered.

"Well, it's about time. We called hours ago about this obstinate little monster defying my rules," she said to me with an angry tone to her voice.

"Really, what rules has he broken?" I asked, looking at the woman who I thought could pass for Cinderella's wicked stepmother.

"I caught him looking in one of the girl's rooms, and when I confronted him, he lied to me. Two rules broken, but there's more. I told him his punishment for lying and being sneaky would be no snack tonight and he would not get to sleep in his own room. He started to yell at me and told me he wasn't a liar, which I know he is. Then he ran away from me." She was mad and her voice had risen up two decibels at least over the course of her explanation.

"Let me talk with Wesley," I said with her lurking over us. "Alone, please." She went back into the house and slammed the door.

"Okay, Wesley, what is going here?" I said, tilting my head back and looking into his big eyes.

"Nothin' ... I wasn't doing anything. Lila said she had somethin' in her room she wanted to show me. So I went in. There was nothin'. She was just tryin' to get me in trouble."

"Sounds good. I can check with her, if that's okay?" He nodded his head okay.

"Now, what about this running away from the foster mom?" The air was still, and he didn't speak. I looked at him, and down his face ran huge crocodile tears.

"What is wrong, Wes? Did somebody hurt you?" He shook his head no, but the tears kept coming.

"Where are you supposed to sleep, Wesley? You have to tell me."

"On the floor ... in there," he said quietly.

"What? On what floor?"

"In there, under the table on the floor, like a dog," he said.

Oh, I was getting upset now. We take a child
from one abusive home and put him in another?
Not on my watch would I let this continue.

I got up and went into the foster home and spoke with the foster
mother. "Oh really, you put them on the floor with only a blanket,"
I repeated her words. "Thank you," I said and left the house.

"Wesley, I will be right back," I said and went down
to the 7-11 and called the CPS supervisor.

"Get him out of there, and I will file my report in the morning.
Yes, pull him tonight. He will not be sleeping on the floor. They
can put him on a sofa, a cot … anything but the floor." I was angry.

I went back and told Wesley he was being moved to
another family and that I would see him in the morning.
He reached out and hugged me. Emotions … wow …
Wes had something lost deep inside his little heart.

This was the breakthrough that led to the most
awesome therapeutic moment of my career!

After this event at the foster home, Wesley bonded to me and
started talking. He talked so much that I hardly ever had to
ask a question because he was always asking and answering!

Finally, one afternoon when we were at the park
swinging, I asked the biggie question.

"Wes, I need to ask you something."

"Okay."

"How did you get those sores all over your body?"

Oh, … the silence was long. Sure he had been talking to me, but he never talked about bad things or showed much emotion. He was still very detached from anything having to do with emotions or his family. Then he spoke.

"He did it. he burned me. It was supposed to be a game."

"You mean your step-dad did it to you?"

"Yeah, and that's when I knew I was a robot."

"A robot?"

"Yeah, I feel no pain. That's what he told me. We practiced on my hands until I couldn't feel the cigarettes burning me. He just kept drinking and burning cigarettes on me. After he burned me, he'd pour beer on me. I had to stand at attention and be real still. It was a game of seeing how tough I was. I never cried…. I never said anything. He kept doing it till it got dark and he fell asleep. It didn't hurt, 'cause I'm a robot, not a boy. That's what Dan said to me, and I believe it. I don't feel nothin' … and robots feel nothin'," he said all of this, and then stopped talking for the rest of our time together that day.

I was so mad at his step-dad, but we had him. Wesley will never go back there. Not only did the step-dad burn him, but also, his mother failed to protect him…. Hell, she didn't even believe her own son. She had to know those were burns, not bug bites.

We finished our visit, and I took Wesley back to his foster home. He never said good-bye or see you. He just slid out of the car and skip-hopped to the house. I watched him a moment. He still had many of the scars from those burns on his arms and legs. How could a grown person be so cruel? Or should I say, how could someone be so sick?

The final breakthrough with Wesley came one day when we were back in the office, meeting in the playroom. It was terribly hot that day, so we stayed in the air conditioned comfort of the playroom. Wesley played by himself, and then as the time drew close to leave, he asked if I would read some Pinocchio to him. So I got the book and put a chair next to me and began to read. He intently listened. Suddenly, I had an inspiration.

"Wesley, stay put. I have to go get something from the kitchen," I said as I set the book down, ran to the door and called Sue to watch Wes just a moment.

I ran to the kitchen and opened the freezer. Yes, an ice cube tray. I took out the tray and popped an ice cube into a paper towel. I shoved the tray back into the freezer, and then rushed back to the playroom. Sue went back to her office.

I picked up the book again and read how Gepetto wished Pinocchio was his real son, a real boy. Once I read that, I took the ice cube and looked at Wesley.

"Wesley, you believe you are a robot, right?"

"Yep, I am. I feel nothing," he replied back to me with no expression on his face, framed by his curly black hair.

"Let me try something, Wes. Open your hand." He did as I asked and I slipped the ice cube into the palm of his hand. Nothing. He didn't cry, scream or even wince.

"I told you. I don't feel nothin'," he said as he dropped the ice back into my hand.

One last chance, I thought. I took the ice cube and ran it up and down his leg and behind the knee. He jumped straight up and screamed.

"Wheeeeee! That's cold!" he screamed out. Then he covered his mouth with his hand. "I felt the ice cube. I felt the cold." He was smiling and his eyes were alive as the words came out from between his fingers. I was smiling. He began jumping up and down around the playroom.

"Miss Pam, I'm like Pinocchio! I'm a real boy, aren't I?"

I looked at him jumping and laughing. Thank you, tiny ice cube (so much for years of therapy, ha).

"Oh, for sure, Wesley! You are a real boy, not a robot," I answered. "A real boy."

I took Wesley to court several weeks later. My report stated that he should not return to his mother's home because it was not safe, and she still would not believe her son. The judge ruled that he not be sent home but placed with his aunt and uncle in Minnesota.

After the decision, we went outside to meet Wesley's mother before he left for Minnesota. She was sitting on a bench, waiting for us.

"Mom! Mom!" Wesley ran up to his mother. She hugged him. "I'm gonna' miss you, Mom," he said.

I stood to the back of the bench a small ways away, but I could hear their conversation.

"Why did you lie, Wesley? Why?" she said to him.

"But Mom, I told the truth. He burned me. He burned me," he pleaded with her to believe and listen to him.

"No, he didn't. Dan would never hurt you," she said, not hearing anything Wesley said. "You have caused so much trouble, Wesley."

"I am not lying. Why do you love him better than me? He
burned me, Mom. That is the truth," he said one last time,
as tears were beginning to glass over his big beautiful eyes.
"Mommy," he tried to reach for her hand. "Believe me, please."

"Wesley, you are a troublemaker and a little liar.
Now you have to go live with your uncle and aunt.
Your lies are going to get you someday."

She stood up and walked away, as the huge tears
started streaming down Wesley's ashen face.

I walked over to her and said, "Please, listen to
your son. He is trying to tell you something very
important, and he needs you to believe him!"

"He is lying! You hear me!" she screamed in my face.
"My husband would never hurt him ... never!"

I walked back to Wesley, who was standing
there watching his mother walk away.

"Why wouldn't she believe me, Miss Pam? Why didn't
she believe me? He burned me ... he really did."

I took his little hand wet from wiping the tears from
his eyes and we walked to car. It was so very hard
that day to keep my tears from joining his.

EPILOGUE

Is belief a matter of taking sides? Do we always discount what our children have to say, because an adult said it isn't so? A child's view of life is as valid as an adult's, isn't it?

The question of truth is relative, so many say. What is one person's truth may be another's lie. The courts believe you rely on evidence and parents rely on each other. Who do children rely on for truth and justice?

All children seek is to be loved unconditionally and held tight in the night when the monsters come out to get them. Most children want to know they will have the same bed to sleep in each night and a place to call home. Children big and small all seek the same things, I believe. They seek to be safe, loved and listened to. All children I have known want a mother to love them and put a band-aid on their scrapes, hug them and tuck them in at night and tell them they are loved. They want a dad who will be there for them and listen to their stories about the day and protect them from the demons of the night.

I have been haunted by a need to tell the stories of the children I have met over the years, to give them a voice. As I have returned to their lives, I have found common threads that bind their stories together. These children, even though their lives are filled with tribulation, still possess an undying hope. They want to believe good things are possible. They need to believe in forgiveness. They dream of being loved. They ask humble questions only children ask about God. Sometimes they talk clearly and loudly in pain and anger; sometimes, their voices are whispers mixed with whimpers in the night.

The common threads are simple: Love me…
Don't leave me alone…Hold me…Listen to me!
Protect me…Play with me…Eat ice cream with
me… And take me to the park with you!.....
All the stories tell us what our inner adult child knows
– we need to belong to someone…a family,
a community, a town, a country who cares and will
listen to our needs.

After many years of working with children, I
believe it does "take a village to raise a child". We must
stop warehousing the troubled children in America!
The institutions are broken and ill funded.
Our priority concerning child welfare needs to shift
toward creating "Guardian Family Programs" that keep
children in families within their communities.
America must stop building places to put children and start
providing "Guardian Families" for children within their own
communities. But this is another story for another book.

Remember from their stories these things –
Children need safe families.….Children need to know
they belong ….. Children need love and constructive
discipline that is consistent….Children
need faith and stable role models….Children need
to stay within communities they are familiar with….
Children need to play and experience life with adults
who won't abandon them every 8 weeks
or six months….Children need to know Hope is real
not just a four letter word that turns into Lost.
We are the agents of Hope for our children, and
they depend on us to listen to their stories.
We are also the Agents of Change that must provide
a better – safer – stable – loving childhood
for all our children.

ABOUT THE AUTHOR

PAM UHER the author of this compelling group of
stories about children caught in a world of trauma and
chaos has "captured the voice of America's Kids".

Pam grew up during the turbulent 1960's in the Washington,
D.C. area and upstate New York Finger Lakes region.
Educated at Scarritt College, Vanderbilt Divinity School
and Brite Divinity School, when she left the halls of
academic privilege to enter a world of service and social
ministry her life became forever changed by the
children she encountered. She is known as an avid child advocate
around the country and her workshops are creative adventures
 that bring innovative dynamic perspectives to child welfare.

Her journey has taken her through the trenches and underbelly
of various social service agencies designed to rescue and
rehabilitate America's children. From the role of counselor,
teacher, program director, case worker, interventionist and minister
Pam presents composites of real children from her case files.

Broken, battered, angry, addicted, abandoned and abused
kids have been given a forum to speak in this collection
of often raw and touching moments from their lives.
As one editor said, "I couldn't stop reading....
and when I reached the last page I wanted to know more."

Pam states many times in the book that children from all
types of backgrounds and circumstance ask a common question:
"Why doesn't anybody listen to me...really listen?" It is her core
conviction in telling these stories that children know what is
wrong in their lives and they know what they need to make
it better! Unfortunately the adult world does not always
"listen....or really hear" children when they speak,
play, draw, dream and whisper in the dark.